Handbook of Comparative Education Law

Books Previously Published by Charles J. Russo

Primer on Legal Affairs for the School Business Official
Key Legal Issues for Schools: The Ultimate Resource for School Business Officials
The Educational Rights of Students: International Perspectives on Demystifying the Legal Issues
What's the Harm? Does Legalizing Same-Sex Marriage Really Harm Individuals, Families or Society?
The Employment Rights of Teachers: Exploring Education Law Worldwide
The Law of Special Education and Non-Public Schools: Major Challenges in Meeting the Needs of Youth with Disabilities
God vs. Darwin: The War between Evolution and Creationism in the Classroom
The Legal Rights of Students with Disabilities: International Perspectives
Key Legal Issues for Schools: The Ultimate Resource for School Business Officials, 2nd Edition
Handbook of Comparative Higher Education Law
Global Interest in Student Behavior: An Examination of International Best Practices, Volume 1
International Perspectives on Student Behavior: What We Can Learn, Volume 2
Gravissimum Educationis: Golden Opportunities in American Catholic Education 50 Years after Vatican II
Handbook of Comparative Education Law: Selected Asian Nations, Volume 2

Forthcoming books by Charles J. Russo

Schools and Religion
Religion in American Education: A Legal Encyclopedia
Handbook of Comparative Education Law: Selected European Nations, Volume 3
Handbook of Comparative Education Law: The Americas and Selected African Nations, Volume 4
Student Discipline: An International Problem
The Law of Special Education: A Hands-On Guide for Educators and Parents

Handbook of Comparative Education Law

British Commonwealth Nations, Volume 1

Edited by Charles J. Russo

ROWMAN & LITTLEFIELD
Lanham • Boulder • New York • London

Published by Rowman & Littlefield
A wholly owned subsidiary of
The Rowman & Littlefield Publishing Group, Inc.
4501 Forbes Boulevard, Suite 200, Lanham, Maryland 20706
https://rowman.com

Unit A, Whitacre Mews, 26-34 Stannary Street, London SE11 4AB,
United Kingdom

British Library Cataloguing in Publication Information Available

Library of Congress Cataloging-in-Publication Data

Names: Russo, Charles J., editor.
Title: Handbook of comparative education law. Volume 1, British commonwealth nations / edited by Charles J. Russo.
Description: Lanham : Rowman & Littlefield, [2017] | Includes bibliographical references and index.
Identifiers: LCCN 2017031628 (print) | LCCN 2017032920 (ebook) | ISBN 9781475821697 (Electronic) | ISBN 9781475821673 (cloth : alk. paper) | ISBN 9781475821680 (pbk. : alk. paper)
Subjects: LCSH: Educational law and legislation--Commonwealth countries.
Classification: LCC K3740 (ebook) | LCC K3740 .H36 2017 (print) | DDC 344/.1124107--dc23
LC record available at https://lccn.loc.gov/2017031628

∞ ™ The paper used in this publication meets the minimum requirements of American National Standard for Information Sciences Permanence of Paper for Printed Library Materials, ANSI/NISO Z39.48-1992.

Printed in the United States of America

To
Debbie, my wife,
Emily, my daughter,
Lorelai, my granddaughter

With all of my love and affection, now, always, and forever

Contents

Acknowledgments

As with any book, there are a number of people who must be thanked. Four sets of people in were very helpful in assisting me in putting this book together. First, many thanks to Tom Koerner, vice president and editorial director at Rowman & Littlefield Education, who was most supportive of this project from its inception through its being published. Thanks also to Ms. Emily Tuttle, an assistant editor, and Mr. Chris Fischer, an assistant production editor, for copyediting the text.

Second, it almost goes without saying that I am most grateful to the authors for their valuable contributions to this book.

Third, I would like to thank my assistant, Ms. Elizabeth Pearn at the University of Dayton, for her efforts in copyediting and helping to prepare the final manuscript for publication.

At the University of Dayton, I would like to thank my dean in the School of Education and Health Sciences, Kevin Kelly, my chair in the Department of Educational Administration, Dave Dolph, and my dean in the School of Law, Andrew Strauss, for their ongoing support and encouragement as well as for providing an atmosphere which is to conducive to ongoing research and academic inquiry.

Fourth, but certainly not least, I would like to express my deepest appreciation for my wife Debbie, my daughter Emily, and our granddaughter Lorelai, to whom this book is dedicated, for their ongoing love and support, and without whom none of this work would have been completed.

Introduction

As the world continues to shrink amid growing interdependence, one of the major challenges facing the global community is ensuring the establishment of sound, working school systems designed to produce educated citizenries. The law is a major factor that helps to create educational systems while monitoring their quality as it protects the rights of both teachers and students. Clearly, this is a daunting task for legal systems around the world as they seek to ensure national stability and well-educated citizenries.

The centrality of education on an international level was first highlighted by the promulgation of the Universal Declaration on Human Rights (Declaration) in 1948.[1] In fact, the Declaration was the first internationally accepted document to enunciate the value of education as a basic human right; this recognition has helped to shape not only the nature of school systems but has also helped to define and safeguard the rights of students, their parents, and teachers. According to Article 26 of this Declaration:

1. Everyone has the right to education. Education shall be free, at least in the elementary and fundamental stages. Elementary education shall be compulsory. Technical and professional education shall be made generally available and higher education shall be equally accessible to all on the basis of merit.
2. Education shall be directed to the full development of the human personality and to the strengthening of respect for human rights and fundamental freedoms. It shall promote understanding, tolerance and friendship among all nations, racial or religious groups, and shall further the activities of the United Nations for the maintenance of peace.
3. Parents have a prior right to choose the kind of education that shall be given to their children.

Additionally, a variety of other international and domestic documents, including judicial opinions of the United States Supreme Court and those of high courts in other nations, have recognized the rights not only of students to receive an education but also of the corresponding right addressing the freedom of teachers to teach as they deem fit, free from unwarranted governmental interference. At the same time, there has been incredible growth in the rate at which children attend school in developing nations, necessitating the creation of a body of well-educated teachers who can instruct these students.

Starting with the enactment of compulsory schooling laws for primary schools in the middle of the nineteenth century,[2] especially in Western industrialized nations beginning with the United States, enrollments in elementary and secondary education have grown dramatically. Even so, a 2010 analysis, published in 2013, of 146 nations reveals that among persons fifteen years of age and older, in 1950 47.1 percent lacked any formal education, a number that has declined to 14.55 percent.[3] Moreover, elementary school completion grew from only 17.1 percent to 17.3 percent while those who completed a secondary education did increase from 5.2 percent to 25.9 percent.[4] To this end, a study published by the World Bank noted that the patterns of educational attainment clearly vary greatly across various countries as well as across population groups within these nations.[5]

For some, basic education is practically universal, whereas for others attainment is dismal as the average years of study rose from only 3.12 to 7.89.[6] A value of this proposed volume, then, is that it is designed to provide users with an understanding of how laws in selected countries promote the development of educational systems that can be used in nations where schooling for all is still not a priority.

Concerns over the need for primary and secondary schools, let alone higher education, have emerged as important throughout the world, largely as a consequence of the increasing range of rights accorded citizens in their home countries. While there are similarities in the ways educational institutions operate, there are also many differences. Further, legislative and judicial systems around the world continue to draw increasingly on the knowledge and experience of educational leaders in other countries in order to improve on the quality of schooling in their own countries.

As the first of four books on comparative legal issues in education, this volume joins others I have edited alone or with others on the rights of students, teachers, children with disabilities, student discipline, and the status of higher education; then, this work focuses on issues in elementary or primary and secondary education so as to offer guidance to educational and legislative leaders in other nations.

This book and its companion volumes include original chapters addressing legal issues in nineteen countries on all six inhabited continents. All of the chapters follow the same template to facilitate the study of similarities and differences between and among countries. Even so, the authors were free to add information as they saw fit. All of the chapter authors are leading academicians in education law in the countries about which they have written and most have contributed to other volumes in this series on the rights of students and students with disabilities, the rights of teachers, the status of higher education, and disciplining of students in elementary and secondary schools, thereby enhancing a strong continuity from one volume to the next.

As such, insofar as the purpose of laws are concerned with developing educated citizenries starting with children, this book examines similarities and differences in education laws in four nations which, in varying degrees, share the British commonwealth tradition: Australia, Malaysia, New Zealand, and Singapore, in the hope of enhancing international awareness of the similarities and advantages associated with bringing together knowledge from ten countries concerning various issues in higher education. It is my hope to have this book serve as a valuable resource for academicians, lawyers, and educational practitioners by providing them with an enhanced awareness of strategies that are being used to manage problems commonly faced in multiple educational settings. The authors have taken every effort to demystify the legal complexities and technical language of the law as it related to education law while ensuring that their work is reader friendly.

OVERVIEW OF THIS VOLUME

In light of the uneven status of the education laws in many places, this book includes essays by experts from four nations to address commonalities in this important, and timely, issue. These experts, all of whom are accomplished academics and/or jurists, are Joan Squelch, from Australia; Fatt Hee Tie, from Malaysia; Sally Varnham, from New Zealand; and Mui Kim Teh and Sook May Chia, from Singapore. The four nations examined in this volume were selected because they share a common British Commonwealth and common law heritage. Accordingly, the education law systems in these countries share common features, even as they differ, based on the unique way in which their national heritages developed, thereby allowing for interesting analyses.

Based on a common outline, these experts examined such issues as the nature of their national legal systems, school governance models, instructional issues, the rights of students and teachers, and emerging issues. Acknowledging the ways in which issues vary from one nation to the next, especially in light of their cultural, religious, political, and practical differences, the authors examined the topics as they saw appropriate, presenting them from their own points of view.

By affording chapter authors some latitude as they address the identified topics, it is still possible to draw conclusions in a final chapter that can hopefully lead to future dialogue and study. Further, as noted, recognizing the importance of as far-reaching a representation as possible, I was fortunate to be able to ensure that I had at least one nation on each continent or region of the world represented in the two volumes.

It is my fervent hope that this collection of essays will enhance a common understanding of the status of K–12 education throughout the world. As interdependence grows in a continually shrinking world, then one of the major challenges facing the global community is to observe what goes on in other nations as leaders seek to learn from one another in facing the challenge of preparing educated citizenries for the future.

Readers are advised that rather than translate all notes and other pertinent terms into English, they are occasionally transliterated in their original languages. I have done this not only because the underlying documents are often unavailable in English but also since translating text might create difficulties for native speakers who wish to research relevant materials. In addition, since each of the nations covered in this book uses slightly different systems of legal citation, I have left references in their original form rather than attempt to standardize them under one rubric. Finally, I have preserved minor variations in the different forms of English used throughout the world so that readers can get a flavor of how our seemingly common tongue is used throughout the world, particularly for scholars whose native language is not English.

CONCLUSION

Of course, no single book can ever hope to cover the myriad of legal topics, or laws of nations, addressing the legal status of K–12 education law. Even so, I hope that these informative, thought provoking, well-written and researched chapters, authored by leading scholars in the field, can serve as up-to-date and ready sources of information to help keep educational leaders, academics, and students abreast of the many changes in the ever-growing area of comparative education law.

NOTES

1. Universal Declaration on Human Rights (1948), http://www.un.org/en/documents/udhr/index.shtml/
2. C. J. Russo (2010). "Reflections on Education as a Fundamental Human Right," *Education and Law Journal*, Vol. 18, No. 1, 87–105.
3. R. J. Barro and J. W. Lee (2013). "A New Data Set of Educational Attainment in the World, 1950–2010," *Journal of Development Economics*, Vol. 104, 184–198, table 3. See also

World Bank (2009), Educational Attainment and Enrollment Around the World, http://web.worldbank.org/

4. Ibid.

5. World Bank (2009), Educational Attainment and Enrollment Around the World, http://web.worldbank.org/

6. Barro and Lee supra note 3.

Chapter One

Australia

Joan Squelch

INTRODUCTION

This chapter deals with the system of elementary and secondary education in Australia within a legal context. The chapter provides a brief outline of the nature of the legal system in Australia and its main sources of education law. An explanation follows of the legal positions on various aspects of primary and secondary schooling in Australia in relation to compulsory education and parental duties, school funding and governance, safety and liability in schools, and rights of teachers and students. The chapter includes a brief discussion on the education of refugee and asylum-seeking children as one of the key emerging human rights issues for schools.

AUSTRALIAN LEGAL SYSTEM AND SOURCES OF EDUCATION LAW

The Commonwealth of Australia was formerly established in January 1901 as a federal system under the Commonwealth of Australia Constitution Act 1900 (the Constitution), an act of the Parliament of the United Kingdom.[1] At federation six independent British colonies joined to form a united commonwealth consisting of six independent states and two mainland self-governing territories,[2] each with its own autonomous executive, legislature, and judicial systems.[3]

The Constitution is the highest law of the commonwealth and established the three arms of government based on the doctrines of representative government and the separation of powers. The executive power of the commonwealth is vested in the queen and exercised by the governor-general as the queen's representative.[4] Legislative power of the commonwealth is vested in the federal parliament.[5] The federal parliament is limited in its law-making powers to those powers enumerated in the Constitution. In addition to only a few exclusive powers, the federal parliament has concurrent power with the six states to pass laws on forty-one listed matters.[6] Law-making powers not listed in the Constitution make up the residual powers of the states. The territories are empowered to make laws under their respective self-governing legislation.

The enumerated heads of power do not include education. The states and territories are responsible for establishing, administering, and financing education systems. Therefore, each state and territory jurisdiction has its own raft of education legislation, regulations, and policies. States and territories are mainly responsible for primary and secondary schooling, with increasing involvement by the federal government. Higher education is a shared responsibility between the federal government and states and territories, with the bulk of higher education funding provided by the federal government.[7]

The Constitution further establishes the High Court of Australia while providing for the creation of a system of federal courts that currently includes the Federal Magistrates Courts, the Family Court of Australia, and the Federal Court of Australia, which has wide jurisdiction over various areas of law including higher education, discrimination, consumer protection, and immigration law.[8] The states and territories have their own independent system of courts made up of lower courts (magistrates' courts), intermediate courts (district or county courts), and supreme courts (the highest court in a state or territory).[9]

The primary sources of education law are the respective commonwealth and state constitutions, common law, and statutory law. Common law has its origins in British common law, which was received at the time of colonization and is an unwritten, judge-made law. Common law is the source of important principles of law that inform education law, such as the duty of care and natural justice. Moreover, areas of law such as contract law and tort law are based on common law.

Statutory law is made up of a vast body of legislation and regulations. As noted, States have concurrent power to pass laws with respect to the enumerated law-making powers under the Constitution.[10] Education is a residual power of the states. States and territories also have their own constitutions, which empowers them to make laws with "respect to peace, order and good governance." Hence all jurisdictions have passed laws with respect to education. In addition to general commonwealth, state, and territory laws such as family law, consumer law, discrimination law, employment law, health and safety law, and criminal law that apply to the education context, there is an array of specific primary and subordinate education laws that govern all aspects of the education system within a particular jurisdiction.[11]

Subordinate or delegated legislation is largely made up of regulations respective Ministers of Education are empowered to make under enabling education legislation. Education legislation and regulations are further underpinned by departmental polices and guidelines which provide guidance on the interpretation and implementation of laws. Important policies and guidelines include those that deal with school attendance, student behavior management, student safety, and the supervision of students.

Where there is a conflict between commonwealth law and state law, commonwealth law prevails to the extent of the inconsistency between the laws. This means that a state law remains inoperative until such time as the inconsistency between the laws no longer exists.[12] Under section 122 of the Constitution, commonwealth law also prevails over territory laws.

INSTITUTIONAL ISSUES

Compulsory School Attendance

Schooling is compulsory in all Australian jurisdictions. Although there is some variation among states and territories, generally all children between the ages of five and six are required to enroll in and attend school until the age of sixteen or seventeen. In Western Australia for example, the compulsory education period means "from the beginning of the year in which the child reaches the age of 5 years and 6 months; and until the end of the year in which the child reaches the age of 17 years and 6 months; or the child reaches the age of 18."[13] To meet the compulsory attendance requirement, children may attend government or nongovernment (or private) schools, or may be homeschooled.

Parents therefore have a legal duty to send their children to school. Children who do not attend school on a regular basis are considered to be at risk. In South Australia, for instance, the Child Protection Act 1993 states that a child is at risk "if the child is compulsory school age but has been persistently absent from school without satisfactory explanation of the absence."[14] Therefore, it is an offense not to send a child to school and parents may be fined if they fail to enroll their child in school for the compulsory education period.[15] A children's court may, on application by the education authority, issue a "compulsory school undertaking" directing the parents to comply with compulsory school attendance requirements.[16]

In Western Australia, by way of illustration, the Parent Support and Responsibility Act 2008 makes provision for the Children's Court to make "responsible parenting orders" that may direct parents to "take all reasonable steps to ensure that the child attends school."[17] Children who are living independently must enroll themselves in school; failure to do so in some jurisdictions may lead to action taken against such children.[18] Because legal action is seen as a last resort, generally the relevant education authority must take all reasonable steps to ensure parental compliance with the compulsory schooling provisions before commencing legal action.

Financial Assistance for Schools

Funding of government and nongovernment schools is provided by federal government grants and by the respective state and territory governments which are ultimately responsible for establishing and maintaining a system of public education. Federal funding for government and nongovernment schools, including religious schools, is made through a complex system of financial assistance grants under the Australian Education Act 2013 (Cth).

School funding is underpinned by the principle that the "schooling system be of a high quality and be highly equitable" so that "all students in all schools are entitled to an excellent education."[19] The aim is to support an education system that will "create a highly skilled, successful and inclusive workforce" and one which will "strengthen the economy" and "increase productivity."[20]

Federal funding for government schools is provided directly to states under section 96 of the Constitution and to territories under section 122 of the Constitution, subject to certain conditions.[21] The conditions of financial assistance require states and territories to implement national policy initiatives relating to school education. Conditions include working cooperatively with government and nongovernment authorities to deliver high quality education, improving the quality of teachers, addressing Aboriginal and Torres Strait Islander educational disadvantage, and supporting the work of national educational institutions such as the Australian Curriculum, Assessment and Reporting Authority.[22]

The amount of recurrent funding a school receives depends on whether a school is a "participating"[23] or "non-participating."[24] Financial assistance to participating schools, government and nongovernment, is calculated using a "base amount for all schools" and "loadings" for schools with particular needs.

The base amount is determined with reference to the number of students in a school; the schooling resource standard, an annual indexed amount of funding per student; and a school community's capacity to make a financial contribution.[25] Loadings are determined with reference to the type, size, location, special needs, socioeconomic status, and English proficiency of the school, and the number of Aboriginal and Torres Strait Islander students.[26]

Financial assistance for non-participating schools, which can only be government schools, is determined with reference to the "national specific purpose payment" provided for under the Federal Financial Relations Act 2009 (Cth).[27] Additional discretionary capital funding[28] and "special circumstances funding"[29] may also be provided to improve capital infrastructure and unexpected or emergency situations.

Federal government financial assistance for nongovernment schools is provided directly to the states and territories and then paid to the approved authority for nongovernment schools "as soon as reasonably practicable."[30] Capital funding provided to nongovernment schools under the Capital Grants Program is managed by an authorized "block grant authority." An approved "block grant authority" is a legal entity that is a body corporate for nongovernment schools or a body politic for government schools; conducts a school on a not-for-profit basis; is financially viable; is a fit-and-proper person; and has the required state or territory registration to provide education.[31]

State and territory funding models may vary but are generally based on the needs of a particular school. As an example, Western Australia has a "Student-Centred Funded Model" based on the learning needs of students. All students receive the same allocated amount based on the year level of the student which is supplemented by additional allocations for Aboriginal students, language, disability, social disadvantage, and location requirements.[32]

Primary and secondary education in government schools is free but schools may invite parents to make a voluntary financial contribution to supplement educational programs, resources, and extracurricular activities. Parents may not be compelled to or coerced into making voluntary payments and students may not be discriminated against if parents do not do so.[33] Generally, if a school has a council, it must approve a request for voluntary financial contributions from parents. However, parents are expected to pay for essential educational items such as basic textbooks, stationery, and school uniforms.

Although nongovernment schools receive government funding, most of their funding is derived from student fees and other private sources, including philanthropic bequests. Nongovernment schools charge compulsory school fees which may vary significantly depending on their type and location.

School Governance

In government and nongovernment schools, governance is undertaken by representative school councils or boards made up of the school principal, teachers, parents, community members, and, in limited cases, student representatives.[34] There is generally no legal requirement to include students on a school council. The legal status and functions of government school councils varies across jurisdictions.

School councils in government schools are mandatory in Western Australia,[35] South Australia,[36] the Northern Territory,[37] the ACT,[38] which has school boards, and Tasmania, which has school associations.[39] In Western

Australia, school councils can become incorporated;[40] both incorporated and unincorporated councils may apply to the minister to extend their functions under section 129 of the School Education Act 1999 (WA).[41] In Victoria, all schools are governed by school councils, which are legal entities incorporated under pt 2.3 of the Education and Training Reform Act 2006 (Vic). In New South Wales[42] and Queensland,[43] government schools may establish councils; there is no mandatory requirement.

Functions of school councils are also set out in the respective state and territory education legislation or regulations. The councils do not participate in the day-to-day management of schools. Generally, the functions of councils include providing guidance on the strategic direction and priorities of schools; developing and reviewing school policies; monitoring school performance; allocating funds; encouraging parental involvement; promoting the school in the community; and ensuring the efficient use of resources.[44]

Councils have a significant role to play in the governance of nongovernment schools since most nongovernment schools operate as companies limited by guarantee or incorporated associations, which are common legal structures for non-for-profit organizations. Schools operating as companies limited by guarantee are incorporated under and subject to the Commonwealth Corporations Act 2001. Councils are therefore responsible for ensuring that their schools comply with obligations arising under the corporations law. Importantly, council members have the same legal duties as directors and are obliged to act in the best interest of the school and with due diligence.[45]

Nongovernment schools operating as incorporated associations are established under and subject to the respective state and territory incorporated association legislation under which they have incorporated.[46] Although there is less clarity under the incorporated association legislation about legal duties of members that reflect directors' duties, some jurisdictions have codified the general law duties of good faith and due diligence.[47]

Generally, though, legislation imposes liability of members for noncompliance with obligations under the relevant incorporated association legislation, in particular financial management obligations. In Western Australia, for example, the Associations Incorporation Act 1987 holds that "if a member of the committee of an incorporated association fails to take all reasonable steps to secure compliance by the association with its obligations under this Act, the member commits an offence and is liable to a fine of [A]$500."[48]

Types of Schools

There is a range of different types of government and nongovernment schools. The school system in all jurisdictions consists mainly of pre-primary, primary, and secondary schools. Pre-primary is the first year of compulsory schooling (age five) followed by six years of primary school (years one to six) and six years of secondary schooling (years seven to twelve). In Western Australia, senior colleges specialize in providing an education for students in years eleven and twelve, the final two years of school, and district high schools are generally located in country towns and provide education for students from kindergarten up to year ten or twelve.[49] There are also specialist government and nongovernment schools for students with special education needs.

In most jurisdictions distance education is provided by designated schools which deliver "a schooling service to geographically isolated and other home based students with limited educational choice."[50] This is complemented by the Schools of the Air, which deliver education to children, generally from preschool to year seven, living in remote and isolated areas in Northern Territory, Queensland, New South Wales, South Australia, and Western Australia.[51]

The nongovernment schooling sector is diverse and plays a major role in education in Australia. Nongovernment schools are made up of independent schools, including nonsystemic Catholic schools, and Catholic systemic schools. Catholic systemic schools are administered by Catholic Dioceses and managed by the relevant Catholic schools authorities. Nonsystemic, independent Catholic schools are conducted by Religious Institutes.

According to the Independent Schools Council of Australia, in 2014 independent schools enrolled over 576,000 students or 16 percent of the Australian student population, and Catholic systemic schools enrolled 19 percent of students.[52] Independent schools include a wide variety of religious schools, nondenominational schools, ethnic-based schools, and schools based on a particular education philosophy such as Montessori and Waldorf Steiner schools.

All nongovernment schools are required to be registered in the state or territory in which they are located. Registration requirements may vary between states and territories, but generally nongovernment schools are required to meet certain standards and requirements relating to governance, financial reporting, staffing, premises and facilities, curricula, school safety, and school discipline.[53]

School Safety and Liability

Students have the right to learn in safe school environments. One of the most important duties of school authorities, principals, and teachers is to create and maintain safe school environments, and to take care of the safety and well-being of students. For instance, education legislation states that a key function of a school principal is "to ensure the safety and welfare of students on the school premises; and away from the school premises but on school activities, so far as that can reasonably be done,"[54] and that teachers are "to supervise students and to maintain proper order and discipline on their part."[55]

This is essential for students to be able to learn in a disciplined, positive, and harmonious environment so that they can develop to their full potential. This is emphasized in Australia's "National Safe School's Framework," which aims to ensure that all "schools are safe, supportive and respectful teaching and learning communities that promote student wellbeing."[56]

Duty of Care

In Australia it is well established at common law that principals and teachers owe students a duty of care and that a failure to exercise reasonable care may give rise to liability for negligence.[57] Negligence is described as "conduct by one person that wrongfully and unreasonably causes adverse effects on another."[58] The tort of negligence imposes liability on a person who has a legal duty of care and who breaches that duty by failing to take reasonable care that falls below the standard of care required in circumstances in which it was reasonably foreseeable that there was "not an insignificant risk" that another person may be injured or harmed.[59]

For liability to incur, the person must have suffered some harm factually caused by the negligent conduct of the other person and that the kind of harm caused was reasonably foreseeable.[60]

Australian jurisdictions also have civil liability legislation codifying common law principles of negligence. As at common law, civil liability defines negligence as the "failure to exercise reasonable care and skill."[61] The statutory provisions, which are mostly similar across all jurisdictions, provide that a person, namely the defendant, is not negligent in failing to take precautions against a risk of harm unless the risk was foreseeable (that is, it is a risk of which the person knew or ought to have known), the risk was not insignificant, and a reasonable person in the circumstances would have taken necessary precautions against the risk of harm.[62]

Factors considered in assessing the risk of harm are the probability of harm occurring, the likely seriousness of the harm, the burden of taking precautions to prevent the risk of harm, and the social utility of the activity.[63]

Duty of care in schools involves inter alia ensuring classrooms and playgrounds are safe; students are properly supervised; school safety policies are implemented and monitored; and facilities and equipment are well maintained. Duty of care extends outside of school hours when students are participating in official school activities.

In *Horne v. State of Queensland*,[64] by way of illustration, a school was liable for negligence when a student was seriously injured on their way to take part in a school activity outside the school grounds. The teacher had instructed students to make their way to the tennis courts a short distance from the school. The parents had been assured that students would move in groups accompanied by a teacher. A student decided to borrow a friend's bicycle to ride to the tennis courts. The bicycle had faulty brakes and was apparently too big for her to control. The student lost control of the bike and went under the wheels of a vehicle. The school was liable because the teacher was not in attendance and students had not been adequately supervised.

Supervision is also required before and after school when students are arriving and leaving school.[65] This was established in *Commonwealth v. Introvigne*[66] in which the education authority was liable for failing to provide adequate supervision when a fifteen-year-old boy was injured on school property shortly before class was due to start. The student was swinging on a flagpole in the school quadrangle when a part of the flagpole fell on him, causing serious injury. At the time of the incident there was only one teacher on duty.

In the school context, whether a risk of harm is reasonably foreseeable is determined with reference to factors such as the age of the students, the location, the nature of the activity, and the level of supervision provided. Courts recognize that there are inherent risks in the school environment and that while principals and teachers need to exercise reasonable care and take reasonable steps to provide a safe environment, not every risk is foreseeable or avoidable, and not every risk can be eliminated from the school environment.[67]

For instance, in *Trustees of the Roman Catholic Church for the Diocese of Canberra and Goulburn (as St Anthony's Primary School) v. Hadba*,[68] the school was not liable for an injury sustained by an eight-year-old girl while playing on the flying fox because there were clear safety rules about playing on the flying fox that were reinforced by teachers and there was adequate supervision at the time of the incident.

TEACHER RIGHTS AND DUTIES

Employment of Teachers

The sources of law dealing with the employment of teachers and associated rights and duties are a combination of common law principles of contract, statutory law, and workplace awards and agreements.

Teachers employed in government schools are employees of the Crown and are public servants.[69] Teachers are employed under relevant state and territory statutes,[70] with conditions of employment set out in awards and enterprise agreements that have been negotiated between the respective departments of education and teachers or associations representing teachers.[71] Awards and enterprise agreements cover aspects such as types of employment, salaries, allowances, leave, duties, hours of work, superannuation, probation, promotion, transfers, notice periods, termination, workplace safety, discrimination, and dispute resolution procedures. Employment conditions for teachers in Western Australia are governed by the School Education Act Employees' (Teachers and Administrators) General Agreement 2014.

The terms and conditions of teachers employed in nongovernment schools are similar to those of government school teachers but are determined by the contract of employment between the teachers and their school, and by applicable enterprise agreements negotiated and agreed to between the employing school and staff or staff association, which sets out the minimum conditions of employment. Enterprise agreements in nongovernment schools are generally governed by the federal Fair Work Act 2009.[72]

Teacher Registration

Teachers in all jurisdictions must be registered with the relevant professional teachers' authority before they can be employed as teachers in a government or nongovernment school.[73] All teacher registration authorities are required a keep a register of teachers. Compulsory teacher registration is to ensure the delivery of high-quality education, and to monitor and enforce professional standards and conduct.

Generally, to be registered, teachers must hold a recognized teachers' qualification from an accredited institution, meet the English language proficiency and professional skills requirements, and be a "fit and proper person." Through the policy of mutual recognition, teachers who are registered in one jurisdiction may be eligible to teach in another jurisdiction.

Ongoing teacher registration requires teachers to maintain a high level of professional performance. The national *Australian Professional Standards for Teachers* comprises seven standards that are "grouped into three domains of teaching: Professional Knowledge, Professional Practice and Professional Engagement," which comprehensively describe what teachers should know and be able to do. The standards set out in detail the knowledge, experience, skills, and attributes expected of teachers.[74] Teachers who fail to maintain the required level of professional standards may be terminated from their employment and have their registration suspended or canceled.[75]

In order to meet the requirement of being a "fit and proper person," registration bodies consider aspects such as the criminal history of the person, compliance with registration requirements, and professional conduct.[76] Teachers are therefore required to undergo a criminal record or police check and a "working with children check," which is managed and conducted in accordance with relevant state and territory legislation.[77] In all jurisdictions teachers are required to hold a "working with children card" (working with children clearance notice), which is managed by each state and territory.[78]

Therefore, a teacher who is eligible to teach in one jurisdiction is not necessarily eligible to teach in another Australian state or territory.

Professional Conduct and Discipline

Teachers are expected to demonstrate and maintain high standards of professional conduct. Teachers' professional conduct and discipline are governed by statute and supported by professional codes of practice. For teachers employed in government schools, general obligations and matters pertaining to breaches of discipline and disciplinary procedures are contained in teacher service legislation or public sector management legislation, which provide the statutory framework for the employment and management of the public sector workforce.[79] Teachers employed in nongovernment schools are subject to contractual obligations and the relevant codes of conduct of the employing authority.

In most jurisdictions, the relevant teacher registration authority oversees the professional conduct of registered teachers, and may apply to teachers in government and nongovernment schools. One of the key functions of a teacher registration authority is to ensure that teachers are fit and proper persons and to deal with complaints about teacher conduct. Teacher registration authorities are empowered to receive complaints about teachers, to conduct investigations, and to impose sanctions.[80]

Disciplinary action may be taken against teachers for misconduct, sexual offenses, improperly obtaining registration, failing to comply with a condition of registration, failing to meet the fit and proper person requirement, and for being dismissed by the employer. An employer is required to notify the registration body in writing if a teacher has been suspended, dismissed, or has resigned following an investigation. Teachers are also obliged to notify registration bodies if convicted of offenses or if they failed a working with children check.[81]

Generally, upon receipt of a complaint, the teacher registration authority may conduct a preliminary investigation to determine whether there is a matter to be heard. The teacher registration authority appoints a disciplinary committee to conduct an enquiry and to hold a formal hearing. In the event of a disciplinary investigation, teachers have a right to natural justice and hence a right to a fair hearing and unbiased decision making. In some jurisdictions this is expressly stated in the legislation.[82]

Based on a disciplinary committee's finding, a teacher registration authority can impose sanctions, which can include a caution or warning; a reprimand; a fine not exceeding a prescribed amount;[83] conditions imposed on the registration, suspension, or cancellation of teacher registration; and permanent disqualification from teaching.[84] Appeals against decisions are generally lodged with the relevant state administrative tribunal or administrative division of a local district court.[85]

Rights and Freedoms

Australia has no constitutionally entrenched bill of rights; therefore, rights and freedoms are to be found in statute and common law.[86] The Constitution provides a limited implied right to freedom of political communication derived from the principles of responsible and representative government and hence the right to participate in political discourse.[87] There is also no express or independent right to freedom of association, which is regarded as a corollary to the implied right to political communication. However, the importance and value of freedom of association in a democratic society is recognized, and commonwealth, state, or territory industrial laws protect the right of workers, including teachers, to freely associate by joining unions and professional associations.[88]

Section 116 of the Constitution provides for the free exercise of religious belief. Even so, this is not a personal right; the provision merely limits the law-making powers of the federal parliament insofar as the "Commonwealth shall not make any law for establishing any religion, or for imposing any religious observance, or for prohibiting the free exercise of any religion, and no religious test shall be required as a qualification for any office or public trust under the Commonwealth."

Therefore section 116 allows for the establishment of religious schools and the exercise of religious practices in government and nongovernment schools.[89] Moreover, in terms of anti-discrimination, teachers may not be discriminated against on the basis of religious beliefs and practices, unless an exemption for religious schools apply legislation; this is discussed below.

In Australia there is no constitutional right or general legal right to privacy.[90] In terms of statutory law, there is some protection of personal data. The Commonwealth Privacy Act 1988, which is overseen by the Office of the Australian Information Commissioner, applies to federal government agencies and organizations, and certain private entities, including nongovernment schools with an annual turnover that exceeds A$3 million. The Privacy Act contains thirteen Privacy Principles regulating the way organizations collect, store, provide access to, use, and disclose personal information.[91] Most states and territories have similar legislation to protect the use of personal data by organizations, which applies to state and territory government education departments and government schools.[92]

Discrimination Issues

In addition to specific federal anti-discrimination legislation,[93] all states and territories in Australia have anti-discrimination or equal opportunity laws covering employment in the education sector.[94] There is some overlap between the commonwealth and state or territory legislation; these operate concurrently so a person can choose the jurisdiction in which to bring a complaint about discrimination. A person is required to comply with both commonwealth and the respective state or territory anti-discrimination laws.

Across all jurisdictions, teachers and principals have a right not to be directly and indirectly discriminated against on the basis of various prohibited grounds, including age, disability, race, nationality, ethnicity, gender, sexual orientation, marital status, pregnancy, breastfeeding, political affiliation, and religious belief.[95]

Religious educational institutions may be exempt from some anti-discrimination provisions. Generally, it is not unlawful for religious schools to discriminate on the basis of religious beliefs in relation to the employment of teachers where the school is conducted in accordance with the doctrines, tenets, beliefs, or teachings of a particular religion and in order to "avoid injury to the religious susceptibilities of adherents of that religion or creed."[96] There is no exemption from discrimination based on race and disability.

Complaints about discrimination are, at first instance, dealt with through a process of conciliation. A complainant may lodge a complaint with a state or territory body under the relevant legislation,[97] or under federal legislation with the Australian Human Rights Commission (AHRC). The role of the AHRC is to receive and investigate complaints, and to help the parties resolve the complaint through an informal, nonlegal process of conciliation. The parties may be assisted by a support person and in some situations a legal representative. The conciliation process may result in various outcomes including an apology, a statement acknowledging a person's hurt and embarrassment, a change of policy or compensation.[98]

By way of illustration, a teacher who was employed in a nongovernment school had taken a period of maternity leave and on her return requested part-time work for a specific period. The teacher claimed that when she requested to return to her original full-time position and work, she was told it no longer existed because of a drop in enrollment numbers and changes to teaching arrangements. The teacher claimed she had been discriminated against on the basis of sex. The matter was resolved with the teacher agreeing to accept a redundancy payment and the educational institution agreeing to provide the teacher with a work reference and to revise its procedures in relation to maternity leave to address the issues raised in the complaint.[99]

If the parties are unable to resolve a matter, the president of the AHRC issues a certificate terminating the matter. The complainant may then institute legal proceedings in the Federal Court of Australia or the Federal Magistrates Court.

STUDENT RIGHTS AND DUTIES

Admission to Schools

As noted above, because it is compulsory for school-age children to attend school, their parents have a legal duty to ensure that their young are enrolled in government or nongovernment schools, or have permission to school them at home. Students who meet the general admission requirements may not be discriminated against on grounds of gender, sexual orientation, race, religion, and/or disability, unless a lawful exemption applies, for example, in the cases of single-sex schools, religious schools, and/or special needs schools.[100]

The school admission process for government schools is set out in education laws, regulations, and policy guidelines based on principles of equal access and non-discrimination. School admission requirements generally concern a child's age, Australian citizenship or visa status, and residential qualification. Children are required to attend schools designated for particular residential areas. A school principal may in some circumstances enroll a child from outside the residential intake area if an appropriate educational program is available and there is classroom accommodation.[101]

A school must keep a register of school enrollments. A student's enrollment may be cancelled if it has been obtained based on false information, a child's place of residence has changed, or the educational program is no longer available.

Students are required to provide an "Immunisation Status Certificate" issued by the Australian Childhood Immunisation Register, which details the history of their immunization, when they apply for admission to a primary school.[102] An unimmunized student may generally not be refused enrollment but may be instructed to stay at home in the event of an outbreak of a vaccine-preventable disease. In terms of infectious diseases, the Disability Standards for Education provide that it is not unlawful for a school to "isolate, or discriminate against" a student with an infectious disease in order to protect the health or well-being of other students.[103]

Discipline and Natural Justice

School principals and teachers have a legal duty to maintain orderly and safe school environments while managing student behavior. All schools are required to have student behavior management plans. Education legislation and policy provide for a range of statutory disciplinary sanctions that may be used when students breach school rules. These include detention, time-out, community service, suspension, and exclusion (expulsion). Corporal punishment is prohibited.[104]

Suspension and exclusion from school are used for cases of serious breaches of discipline. For instance, a student may be excluded from school for behavior adversely affecting or threatening the safety of any person, prevents another student from participating in an educational program of the school, or results in damage to property.

Education legislation and regulations, which vary across jurisdictions, prescribe basic principles, authority, grounds, requirements, and procedures for suspending or excluding a student from a government school. Importantly, students in government schools have a right to natural justice (due process). Students are therefore entitled to a fair hearing (an opportunity to put their case) and an impartial, unbiased decision. Provision is made for students or their parents to be consulted and notified in writing of the proposed suspension or exclusion, prior to the action coming into effect. In addition to this notification, parents are provided with the guidelines and procedures on suspension and exclusion.[105]

To be afforded a fair hearing, students must be informed about the nature of the allegations, the basis for the allegations, and possible outcomes. A fair hearing requires disclosing all the relevant material on which the allegations are based and which will be relied on to make a decision.[106] Students must also be given written notice about the date and time of the hearing and the process, and to be advised of their right to be assisted by a support person, usually a parent but also a teacher or fellow student.[107]

Generally, a student is entitled to natural justice before being suspended. However, a student may be suspended with immediate effect in situations where the student is posing a serious threat to others, for example, being in possession of a dangerous weapon or being physically violent.[108]

The law does not require nongovernment schools to apply natural justice. For students in nongovernment schools, disciplinary procedures are generally governed by the contracts between the parents and the schools which do not need to make provision for natural justice. However, all nongovernment schools are required to be registered and they are required to have appropriate student management policies and processes in place as part of the requirements for registration.[109]

Searches, Seizures, and Drug Testing

As noted, school officials have a duty to provide safe and orderly environments while caring for the health and well-being of students. This duty arises under common law and education legislation as well as work health and safety legislation.

In the interest of student safety and well-being, school behavior management policies may therefore provide for students to be searched and items seized from students if there are reasonable grounds to believe the student is in possession of a prohibited item. Mobile phones, iPads, and other such devices may also be seized if they contain illegal or offensive material or if they are being used inappropriately. Yet there is no general common law power to conduct searches.[110]

The powers to conduct student searches may be derived expressly or impliedly from education legislation or regulations in each jurisdiction. For example, in South Australia the school principal (head teacher) or a person authorized by the principal may search school premises and "any bag, locker or other receptacle" used by any person receiving an education at the school to safeguard the loss of property used in the process of instruction.[111]

Victoria also expressly provides that a principal, an assistant principal, or an authorized teacher may search for and seize harmful items. Searches may be conducted of the school premises as well as vehicles, bags, and storage spaces used by students in the course of official teacher supervised activities.[112]

In Western Australia a member of the teaching staff at a government school may confiscate a student's property if the item concerned is used on the school's premises in a manner that is likely to disrupt good order, adversely affect the safety or welfare of persons, or cause damage to property on the school's premises.[113] If a student refuses a reasonable request to hand over property they may be subject to school discipline measures, which may include suspension from school in the case of serious breaches of policy and rules.

School officials face the ongoing challenge of managing drug and alcohol use among students. These educators have the duty of care to protect the health and safety of students, and to take reasonable steps to ensure that they are not harmed by the supply or use of drugs. School principals are responsible for communicating and implementing policy and procedures for managing drug-related incidents in schools. Government schools do not have the power to test students for drugs, including breathalyzer tests, at school or during school activities. However, school authorities may require students to undergo drug tests and provide medical reports as pre-conditions for inclusion in, for example, sports programs.[114] Nongovernment school polices, on the other hand, may provide for drug testing.

Education departments provide policy guidelines for school officials on how to plan for and manage the use of alcohol, tobacco, prescription drugs, performance-enhancing drugs, and illicit drugs at schools and during off-campus school activities. Policies also focus on implementing education programs aimed at preventing substance abuse.[115] Moreover, a school behavior management plans and the disciplinary measures of suspension and exclusion would apply. Students have a right to natural justice (as discussed above) when investigated for breaching the policies and rules of their schools on drug and alcohol use. Principals are generally required to report incidents involving the illegal use, possession, or distribution of drugs at school to the police.[116]

Freedom of Religion

There is no personal constitutional right to religious freedom in Australia but at common law students have a right to freedom of religion, thought, and conscience.[117] Moreover, Australia is a signatory to various international human rights conventions including the Convention on the Rights of the Child, which protects the right to religious freedom.[118]

Further, subject to reasonable limitations and permissible exemptions in the case of private religious schools, students may not be discriminated against on the basis of their religious beliefs and practices in terms of access to education, participation in education programs, and the delivery of education services.[119]

Public education in Australia is secular.[120] Even so, schools may conduct voluntary religious education classes, religious activities, and celebrations during the school year. A distinction is usually made between general religious education focusing on the "major forms of religious thought and expression characteristic of Australian society and other societies in the world" and special religious education about particular religions based on "distinctive religious tenets and beliefs," which is provided by specific church or religious groups.[121]

Legislative provisions dealing with religious education and activities in schools varies across jurisdictions but commonly relate to the nature of religious instruction, curriculum matters, hours for instruction, who may teach religious education, and the rights of parents to give notice to a school to withdraw their children from all religious activities.[122] In some jurisdictions, if a school has a council, the principal is obliged to consult it on a general policy concerning the use of prayers, songs, and religious material in school activities.[123]

Freedom of Expression and Speech

At common law students have a right to freedom of expression but there is no constitutional right to freedom of expression or speech in Australia.[124] There is, though, an implied right to freedom of political communication based on principles of responsible and representative government.[125] Therefore, besides a common law right to free speech, students' political communication is protected, which may be subject to reasonable limitations within the school context.

Freedom of expression manifested in dress codes and appearance is one contentious and challenging area for schools, especially in relation to hairstyles, accessories, and body piercings. Schools may develop and enforce policies and reasonable school rules on dress codes and personal appearance. Breaches of these rules are dealt with according to school behavior management policies.[126]

School policies on dress code and appearance are developed in consultation with parents and students, and must take into account financial considerations, health and safety, and anti-discrimination legislation. In terms of antidiscrimination legislation, students may not be discriminated against on grounds of religion, race, and/or ethnicity and, therefore, subject to reasonable limitations, may wear clothing and accessories for religious or cultural purposes.

The Victorian Equal Opportunity Act 2010, for example, states that an "educational authority may set and enforce reasonable standards of dress and appearance for students" and that "standards of dress and appearance for students is considered reasonable when the views of the school community have been taken into account in setting the standard."[127]

Students with Special Needs

All students have a right to education including equal access to educational facilities, services, and programs.[128] Education in Australia is based on the principles of inclusive education and the integration of students with special needs within mainstream schools.[129] In addition, though, each jurisdiction has various separate dedicated public and private schools with specialist facilities for students with particular disabilities and educational needs. There are also educational support centers that provide specialist services, facilities, and equipment for students and families.

It is unlawful for educational providers to discriminate against students on the basis of their disability in education and enrollment in schools.[130] The Disability Standards for Education (Standards),[131] which apply to both government and nongovernment schools, state that students with disabilities have the same rights as other children and that they must be "treated with dignity and enjoy the benefits of education and training in an educationally supportive environment."[132]

The Standards aim to ensure that students with disabilities are able to access and participate in education on the same basis as other students. The Standards set minimum obligations relating to student enrollment (pt 4), participation, curriculum development, accreditation, and delivery of educational programs, student support services, and the elimination of harassment and victimization.

The Standards require school authorities to "reasonably accommodate" students with disabilities by making reasonable adjustments so that they can access and participate in the educational program and school activities. This includes modifying educational programs, changing modes of course delivery, modifying or providing specialist equipment, providing alternative assessments, providing support staff and teacher aides, and modifying educational premises.[133]

EMERGING ISSUE

One of the most significant human rights issues for schools is the education of refugee and asylum-seeker children.[134] Under Australian law, noncitizens who enter the country without valid visas must be detained, including children, until they are granted visas or are removed from the country.[135] Most children in immigration detention have arrived by boat and are detained with adults in offshore or onshore detention facilities.[136]

According to statistics published by the Department of Immigration and Border Protection, at the end of 2015, 91 children were held in closed immigration detention facilities and 329 in community detention. Another 3,983 children are on bridging visas awaiting the outcome of applications for valid visas.[137] Asylum seeker and refugee children who have been granted a bridging visa or protection visa have a right to attend school.[138] There are also a large number of refugee children who arrive in Australia with a valid visa who have to transition into school. For example, public schools in New South Wales enroll between 1,000 and 1,500 newly arrived students from refugee backgrounds each year.[139]

Refugee children in the community and in detention centers face significant challenges when it comes to education and need a high level of support. For children in detention, some schooling is provided in the detention center or in local schools, which in the case of offshore locations are often poorly resourced and unable to meet the needs of asylum-seeker children.[140]

As noted by the Road to Refuge foundation "most refugee children have had disrupted or no education prior to arrival in Australia."[141] Refugee children face many difficulties in terms of communication and cultural barriers, underdeveloped literacy and numeracy skills, lack of prior education experience and adjusting to formal education, health issues, discrimination, and generally adjusting to a new environment.[142] In most jurisdictions the education departments, in partnership with different support services, assist schools and refugee children who are transitioning into formal schooling in Australia.[143]

CONCLUSION

The Australian education system is highly complex and is governed by common law and a vast body of statutory law that includes general law and specific education law. The establishment and provision of education is primarily the responsibility of each state and territory, each with its own system of school education and legal framework. However, national initiatives relating to school funding, the National Safe Schools Framework, and the national standards for dealing with the professional conduct of teachers aim to ensure that there is some uniformity across jurisdictions on matters of national importance.

Ongoing challenges and priorities for school education include school funding and the safety and well-being of teachers and students. Schools also face the challenge of providing safe and supportive learning environments for increasing numbers of refugee and asylum-seeker children who have significant hurdles to overcome in adjusting to a new country and school environments, especially if they have lost multiple years of schooling in their home countries and have been traumatized by being detained in closed detention facilities.

NOTES

1. Commonwealth of Australia Constitution Act (1900) became law on 9 July 1900 and entered into force on 1 January 1901.

2. Unlike the states, the powers of the territories are defined in commonwealth laws. In terms of § 121 of the Constitution, territories can become states with the approval of the federal parliament.

3. New South Wales, Queensland, South Australia, Tasmania, Victoria, Western Australia, Northern Territory, and the Australian Capital Territory (ACT). There are also a number of offshore territories governed by the commonwealth government, as well as Norfolk Island, which is an offshore territory with limited self-government: Department of Infrastructure and Development, Australian Government, *Australian Territories*, http://regional.gov.au/territories.

4. Constitution § 61.

5. Ibid § 1.

6. Ibid § 51.

7. See Sally Varnham, Patty Kamvounais and Joan Squelch (eds), *Higher Education and the Law* (The Federation Press, 2015).

8. Constitution §§ 75–77.

9. Tasmania and Northern Territory have a Supreme Court and Magistrates Courts.

10. Section 51 of the Constitution lists forty heads of power including the addition of § 51xxiiiA, in terms of which the commonwealth can legislate for the "peace, order and good government of the Commonwealth."

11. The primary pieces of legislation establishing and governing the school education systems in each jurisdiction are: Education Act 2004 (ACT); Education Act 1990 (NSW); Education Act 2015 (NT); Education (General Provisions) Act 2006 (Qld); Education Act 1972 (SA); Education Act 1994 (Tas); Education and Training Reform Act 2006 (Vic); School Education Act 1999 (WA).

12. Constitution § 109.

13. Education Act 2004 (ACT) §§ 9–10; Education Act 1990 (NSW §§ 21B–22); Education Act 2015 (NT) §§ 38–40; Education (General Provisions) Act 2006 (Qld) § 9, §§ 176–177; Education Act *1972* (SA) § 75; Education Act 1994 (Tas) § 4; Education and Training Reform Act 2006 (Vic) § 2.1.1; School Education Act 1999 (WA) s 9.

14. Child Protection Act 1993 (SA) § 6(2)(d).

15. Education Act 2004 (ACT) § 10A § 17A; Education Act 1990 (NSW) § 23; Education Act 2015 (NT) § 39; Education (General Provisions) Act 2006 (Qld) § 176; Education Act 1972 (SA) § 75(5); Education Act 1994 (Tas) § 4; Education and Training Reform Act 2006 (Vic) § 2.1.2, § 2.1.23; School Education Act 1999 (WA) s 9(2). In Western Australia a fine of A$2,500 may be imposed.

16. See, for example, Education Act 1990 (NSW) § 22D.

17. Parent Support and Responsibility Act 2008 (WA) § 14.

18. See, for example, Education Act 2013 (NT) § 20A(2).

19. Preamble to the Australian Education Act 2013 (Cth).

20. Ibid.

21. Australian Education Act 2013 (Cth) § 4.

22. Ibid § 22(1).

23. Ibid § 4: A "participating school" is a government or nongovernment school of a state or territory that is party to the National Education Reform Agreement and has a bilateral agreement with the commonwealth government to implement the NERA.

24. Ibid § 4: A "non-participating school" is a government school and funding is determined by reference to the amount of funding non-participating states and territories received during a specified year under the Federal Financial Relations Act 2009 (Cth).

25. Ibid § 31.

26. Ibid § 31.

27. Ibid § 64.

28. Ibid § 67.

29. Ibid § 69.

30. Ibid § 23(3).

31. Ibid pt 5, pt 6.

32. Department of Education, Government of Western Australia, Student-Centred Funding Model, http://www.education.wa.edu.au/home/detcms/navigation/about-us/programs-and-initiatives/student-centred-funding-model/ (4 November 2015).

33. Education (General Provisions) Act 2006 (Qld) § 56; Education and Training Reform Act 2006 (Vic) § 2.2.7.

34. See, for example, Education Act 2004 (ACT) § 41; School Education Act 1999 (WA) § 99.

35. School Education Act 1999 (WA) § 125 unless the Minister exempts a school from having a council.

36. Education Act 1972 (SA) § 83(1).

37. Education Act 2015 (NT) § 103.

38. Education Act 2004 (ACT) § 38.

39. Education Act 1994 (Tas) § 26.

40. School Education Act 1999 (WA) § 130. An incorporated school council may obtain funds for the school but may not borrow money.

41. Additional functions are to take part in the selection of, but not the appointment of, the school principal or any other member of the teaching staff and to carry out any other function prescribed by the regulations for the purposes of § 129.

42. Education Act 1990 (NSW) § 36.

43. Education (General Provisions) Act 2006 (Qld) § 79.

44. Education Act 2004 (ACT) § 38–39; Education Act 1990 (NSW) § 36; Education Act 2015 (NT) § 107; Education (General Provisions) Act 2006 (Qld) § 79, § 81; Education Act 1972 (SA) § 83, § 85; Education Act 1994 (Tas) § 26, § 27; Education and Training Reform Act 2006 (Vic) § 2.3.5; School Education Act 1999 (WA) § 128, § 133.

45. Corporations Act 2001 (Cth) § 180, § 181.

46. For example, nongovernment schools in Western Australia operating as an incorporated association are established under the Associations Incorporation Act 1987 (WA).

47. Associations Incorporation Act 2009 (NSW) §§ 32–33; Associations Incorporation Act 1985 (SA) § 39A.

48. Associations Incorporation Act 1987 (WA) § 42.

49. Department of Education, Government of Western Australia, *Types of Schools*, http://det.wa.edu.au/schoolsandyou/detcms/navigation/your-childs-education/types-of-public-schools/ (4 November 2015).

50. Department of Education and Training, Government of Queensland, *Distance Education*,http://education.qld.gov.au/curriculum/distance/ (4 November 2015).

51. Government of Australia, *Schools of the Air and Remote Learning*, http://www.australia.gov.au/about-australia/australian-story/school-of-the-air (4 November 2015). Teaching and learning is conducted via online conferencing satellite technology and correspondence material.

52. Independent Schools Council of Australia, http://isca.edu.au/about-independent-schools/ (4 November 2015).

53. Education Act 2004 (ACT) § 82, § 88; Education Act 1990 (NSW) § 47; Education Act 2015 (NT) § 124, § 125; Education Act 1994 (Tas) § 51, § 53; School Education Act 1999 (WA) § 154, § 159, § 160.

54. School Education Act 1999 (WA) § 63.

55. School Education Act 1999 (WA) § 64.

56. Department of Education and Training, Australian Government, *National Safe Schools Framework*, https://www.education.gov.au/national-safe-schools-framework-0 (5 November 2015).

57. See, for example, *Geyer v. Downs* (1977) 138 CLR 91; *Ramsay v. Larsen* (1964) 111 CLR 16; *Commonwealth of Australia v. Introvigne* (1982) 150 CLR 258.

58. Julia Davis, *Connecting with Tort Law* (2012, Oxford University Press) 369.

59. Danuta Mendelson, *The New Law of Torts* (2007, Oxford University Press) 238.

60. Ibid.

61. See, for example, Civil Liability Act 2002 (NSW) § 5; Civil Liability Act 1936 (SA) § 3.

62. Civil Law (Wrongs) Act 2002 (ACT) § 43; Civil Liability Act 2002 (NSW) § 5B; Civil Liability Act 2003 (Qld) § 9; Civil Liability Act 1936 (SA) § 32; Civil Liability Act 2002 (Tas) § 11; Wrongs Act 1958 (Vic) § 48; Civil Liability Act 2002 (WA) § 5B.

63. Civil Law (Wrongs) Act 2002 (ACT) § 43(2); Civil Liability Act 2002 (NSW) § 5B(2); Civil Liability Act 2003 (Qld) § 9(2); Civil Liability Act 1936 (SA) § 32(2); Wrongs Act 1958 (Vic) § 48(2); Civil Liability Act 2002 (WA) § 5B(2); Civil Liability Act 2002 (Tas) § 11(2). The common law is applied in the Northern Territory.

64. *Horne v State of Queensland* (1995) Aust Tort Reports 81–343.

65. *Geyer v. Downs* (1977) 138 CLR 91.

66. *Commonwealth of Australia v. Introvigne* (1982) 150 CLR 258.

67. See, for example, *Trustees of the Roman Catholic Church for the Archdiocese of Sydney v. Kondrajian* [2001] NSWCA 308 (24 September 2001) [66]; *Trustees of the Roman Catholic Church for the Diocese of Canberra and Goulburn (as St Anthony's Primary School) v. Hadba* (2005) 221 CLR 161; *Local Spiritual Assembly of the Baha'is of Parramatta Ltd & Anor v. Babak Haghighat* [2004] NSWCA 21 (19 February 2004) [69]; *Swain v. Waverley Municipal Council* (2005) 220 CLR 517 [5].

68. *Trustees of the Roman Catholic Church for the Diocese of Canberra and Goulburn (as St Anthony's Primary School) v. Hadba* (2005) 221 CLR 161.

69. In New South Wales, government school teachers are a part of the government sector and not the public sector.

70. Public Sector Management Act 1994 (ACT); Government Sector Employment Act 2013 (NSW) pt 5, ss 68–70; Public Sector Employment and Management Act (NT); Public Service Act 2008 (Qld); Public Sector Act 2009 (SA); State Service Act 2000 (Tas); Education and Training Reform Act 2006 (Vic); Public Sector Management Act 1994 (WA) pt 5.

71. Awards are instruments applicable to a particular sector and enterprise agreements are instruments that are negotiated between and apply to a particular employer and employees.

Awards and enterprise agreements may operate in conjunction with each other but enterprise agreements generally prevail if there are conflicts between the instruments.

72. Fair Work Act 2009 (Cth) pts 2–4. This act is the national system of workplace law and applies to organizations in the private and nongovernment sector. It applies to not-for-profit associations incorporated in most states and territories and hence many nongovernment schools that operate and incorporated associations.

73. ACT Teacher Quality Institute Act 2010; Teacher Accreditation Act 2005 (NSW); Teacher Registration (Northern Territory) Act (NT); Education (Queensland College of Teachers) Act 2005 (Qld); Teachers Registration and Standards Act 2004 (SA); Teachers Registration Act 2000 (Tas); Education and Training Reform Act 2006 (Vic); Teacher Registration Act 2012 (WA).

74. Australian Institute for Teaching and School Leadership, Standards http://www.aitsl.edu.au/australian-professional-standards-for-teachers/standards/list.

75. Above note 73.

76. Teacher Registration Act 2012 (WA) § 24.

77. See, for example, Teacher Registration Act 2012 (WA) § 43.

78. Working with Vulnerable People (Background Checking Act) 2011 (ACT); Child Protection (Working with Children) Act 2012 (NSW); Care and Protection of Children Act (NT); Working with Children (Risk Management and Screening) Act 2000 (Qld); Children's Protection Act 1993 (SA); Working with Children Act 2005 (Vic); Registration to Work with Vulnerable People Act 2013 (Tas); Working with Children (Criminal Record Checking) Act 2004 (WA).

79. Above note 70.

80. Education (Queensland College of Teachers) Act 2005 (Qld) Ch 5; Teachers Registration and Standards Act 2004 (SA) pt 7; Teachers Registration Act 2000 (Tas) pt 4 div 2; Education and Training Reform Act 2006 (Vic) pt 2.6, which is administered by the Victorian Institute of Teaching; Teacher Registration Act 2012 (WA) pt 5.

81. Below n 84.

82. Teacher Registration and Standards Act 2004 (SA) § 42; Teacher Registration Act 2000 (Tas) § 22B.

83. Teacher Registration Act 2012 (WA) § 70(1)(c).

84. ACT Teacher Quality Institute Act 2010 §§ 63–65; Teacher Accreditation Act 2005 (NSW) § 24A, S 24B; Teacher Registration (Northern Territory) Act (NT) § 64; Education (Queensland College of Teachers) Act 2005 (Qld) § 48, § 56; Teachers Registration and Standards Act 2004 (SA) § 38; Teachers Registration Act 2000 (Tas) § 18A; Education and Training Reform Act 2006 (Vic) § 2.6.27; Teacher Registration Act 2012 (WA) § 70.

85. See, for example, Teachers Registration and Standards Act 2004 (SA) § 49.

86. For example, anti-discrimination legislation. Victoria and the ACT are the only jurisdictions that have a character of rights: Charter of Human Rights and Responsibilities Act 2006 (Vic) and Human Rights Act 2004 (ACT).

87. The seminal case is *Lange v. Australian Broadcasting Corporation* (1997) 189 CLR 520.

88. Under the General Protections of the Fair Work Act 2009 (Cth), employees may choose to join an industrial association and they are protected from adverse action for being a member and participating in lawful industrial activities.

89. See *Williams v. The Commonwealth* (2012) 248 CLR 156 in which it was held that a funding agreement between the Commonwealth of Australia and Scripture Union Queensland for the provision of chaplaincy services at a state school in Queensland was invalid.

90. In *Australian Broadcasting Corporation v. Lenah Game Meats* (2001) 208 CLR 199 the High Court fell short of recognizing a right to privacy but recognized the possibility of a new tort of invasion of privacy.

91. Privacy Act 1988 (Cth) § 13, cch 1.

92. Western Australia does not have privacy legislation but privacy principles are found in the Freedom of Information Act 1992 (WA).

93. Australian Human Rights Commission Act 1986 (Cth); Racial Discrimination Act 1975 (Cth); Sex Discrimination Act 1984 (Cth); Disability Discrimination Act 1992 (Cth); Age Discrimination Act 2004 (Cth).

94. Discrimination Act 1991 (ACT); Anti-Discrimination Act 1977 (NSW); Anti-Discrimination Act 1996 (NT); Anti-Discrimination Act 1991 (Qld); Equal Opportunity Act 1984 (SA); Anti-Discrimination Act 1998 (Tas); Equal Opportunity Act 2010 (Vic); Equal Opportunity Act 1984 (WA).

95. Ibid.

96. Discrimination Act 1991 (ACT) § 33; Anti-Discrimination Act 1996 (NT) § 30; Anti-Discrimination Act 1991 (Qld) § 41; Equal Opportunity Act 1984 (SA) does not include religion as a ground of discrimination but provides for an exemption in relation to religious dress and appearance, § 85zn; Anti-Discrimination Act 1998 (Tas) § 51A; Equal Opportunity Act 2010 (Vic) § 83; Equal Opportunity Act 1984 (WA) § 73. New South Wales legislation does not specially include religion as a protected ground of discrimination.

97. See, for example, the complaints process under the Equal Opportunity Commission of Western Australia http://www.eoc.wa.gov.au/; the Anti-Discrimination Board of New South Wales http://www.antidiscrimination.justice.nsw.gov.au/; Australian Capital Territory Human Rights Commission http://hrc.act.gov.au/.

98. Australian Human Rights Commission, *Complaints Process* https://www.humanrights.gov.au/complaints/complaint-guides/complaint-process.

99. Australian Human Rights Commission, *Conciliation Register* (January to June 2001) https://www.humanrights.gov.au/conciliation-register-sex-discrimination-act-1984-complaints-conciliated-and-finalised-period-jan.

100. Above note 94.

101. Education Act 2004 (ACT) § 10; Education Act 1990 (NSW) § 34; Education Act 2015 (NT) § 39; Education (General Provisions) Act 2006 (Qld) § 115; Education Act 1972 (SA) § 75; Education Act 1994 (Tas) § 19; Education and Training Reform Act 2006 (Vic) § 2.2.13, § 2.2.14, § 2.2.18; School Education Act 1999 (WA) s 16, § 76.

102. See, for example, School Education 1999 (WA); Public Health Act 2010 (NSW).

103. Disability Standards for Education § 10.4.

104. Education Act 2004 (ACT) § 7(4); Education Act 1990 (NSW) § 35(2A), § 47; Education Act 2015 (NT) s 160; Education Act 1994 (Tas) s 82A; Education Training and Reform Act 2006 (Vic) § 4.3.1(6); Education and Training Reform Regulations 2007 (Vic) reg 14; School Education Regulations 2000 (WA) s 40(2). Queensland and South Australia have repealed provisions allowing corporal punishment.

105. Education Act 2004 (ACT) § 36; Education Act 1990 (NSW) § 35; Education Act 2015 (NT) §§ 91–93; Education (General Provisions) Act 2006 (Qld) § 283–85; Education Regulations 2012 (SA) regs 44–45; Education Act 1994 (Tas) § 38; Education and Training Reform Act 2006 (Vic) § 2.2.19; School Education Act 1999 (WA) § 90–94. See also Department of Education and Communities, Government of New South Wales, Suspension and Expulsion of School Students Procedures 2011.

106. *X v. University of Western Sydney* [2014] NSWSC 82 (17 February 2014) (Hall J, 180).

107. *CF (by her tutor JF) v State of New South Wales* (2003) 58 NSWLR 135 [31].

108. See, for example, Department of Education and Communities, Government of New South Wales, Suspension and Expulsion of School Students Procedures 2011 https://www.det.nsw.edu.au/policies/media/media/socialinclusiondownloads/suspol_07.pdf.

109. For example, Education Act 1990 (NSW) § 47. Registration requirements for non-government schools in Northern Territory expressly state that a nongovernment school's policy for the discipline of students must include procedural fairness: Education Act 2015 (NT) § 125(n).

110. Jim Jackson and Sally Varnham, *Law for Educators. School and University Law in Australia* (Sydney: LexisNexis, 2007) 280.

111. Education Regulations 2012 (SA) reg 72.

112. Education and Training Reform Act 2006 (Vic) § 5.8A.3, § 5.8A.4, § 5.8A.6.

113. School Education Regulations 2000 (WA) reg 70(1).

114. See, for example, Department of Education, Government of New South Wales, *Drugs in Schools Policy* https://www.det.nsw.edu.au/policies/student_serv/student_welfare/drug_incid/PD20020040.shtml and the Department of Education and Training, Government of Victoria, *Drug Use* http://www.education.vic.gov.au/school/principals/spag/safety/Pages/druguse.aspx.

115. Ibid.

116. Ibid. See also Tasmania Police, *MoU between Schools and Police. Guidelines for Managing Drug-Related Incidents in Tasmanian Schools 2015–2019* http://www.police.tas.gov.au/programs/mou-between-police-and-schools/.

117. Section 116 of the Constitution limits the legislative powers of the commonwealth to pass laws that establish a state religion or for imposing any religious observance, or prohibit the free exercise of any religion.

118. Convention on the Rights of the Child, adopted and opened for signature, ratification and accession by General Assembly resolution 44/25 on 20 November 1989 (entered into force 2 September 1990) http://www.ohchr.org/en/professionalinterest/pages/crc.aspx art 14.

119. Above note 94.

120. Education Act 2004 (ACT) § 28; Education Act 1990 (NSW) § 30; Education (General Provisions) Act 2006 (Qld); Education Act 1972 (SA); Education Act 1994 (Tas); Education and Training Reform Act 2006 (Vic) s 2.2.10; School Education Act 1999 (WA) § 68(1)(a).

121. See, for example, School Education Act (WA) § 66.

122. Education Act 2004 (ACT) § 28, § 29; Education Act 1990 (NSW) § 32; Education Act 2015 (NT) §§ 86–87; Education (General Provisions) Act 2006 (Qld) §§ 76–80; Education Act 1972 (SA) § 102; Education Act 1994 (Tas) § 34; Education and Training Reform Act 2006 (Vic) § 2.2.11; School Education Act 1999 (WA) § 66, § 69.

123. See, for example, School Education Act (WA) § 70.

124. Only two jurisdictions have a human rights Act. The Human Rights Act 2004 (ACT) provides that "everyone has the rights to hold opinions without interference" and "everyone has a right to freedom of expression" (s 16) and the Victorian Charter of Human Rights and Responsibilities Act 2006 likewise provides for the right to freedom of expression (s 15).

125. Above note 87.

126. Education (General Provisions) Act 2006 (Qld) §§ 360–63.

127. Equal Opportunity Act 2010 (Vic) § 42.

128. See, for example, guiding principles of education: Education Act 2004 (ACT) § 7; Education Act 1990 (NSW) § 4; Education Act 2015 (NT) § 4; School Education Act 1999 (WA) § 3.

129. See, for example, Department of Education, Northern Territory, *Philosophy of Inclusion of Students with Disability* http://www.education.nt.gov.au/__data/assets/pdf_file/0005/40694/DoE-Philosophy-of-Inclusion-for-Students-with-Disability-2016-2018.pdf.

130. Disability Discrimination Act 1992 (Cth) § 22.

131. Department of Education and Training, Australian Government, *Disability Standards for Education 2005* https://docs.education.gov.au/documents/disability-standards-education-2005.

132. Department of Education and Training, Australian Government, *Disability Standards for Education 2005 Guidance Notes*, http://docs.education.gov.au/node/16352 p. 42.

133. *Hills Grammar v. Human Rights and Equal Opportunity Commission* (2000) 100 FCR 306; *Hurst v. State of Queensland* [2006] FCAFC 100; *Scott and Bernadette Finney on behalf of Scarlett Finney v. The Hills Grammar School* No. H98/6 in the Human Rights and Equal Opportunity Commission [2000] http://www.hreoc.gov.au/disability_rights/decisions/comdec/2000/DD000080.htm.

134. *Refugees* are defined as a person who is "outside their own country and has a well-founded fear of persecution due to his/her race, religion, nationality, member of a particular social group or political opinion, and is unable or unwilling to return": Convention Relating to the Status of Refugees (and its 1967 Protocol) 1951, art 1. An asylum seeker is a person seeking refugee status. These terms are sometimes used interchangeably.

135. *Migration Act 1958* (Cth) § 189.

136. The main offshore facilities are on Christmas Island, which is an offshore territory located 2,650 kilometers northwest of Perth and is governed by Australia (Christmas Island Act

1958 [Cth]), and Nauru, an independent island in the central Pacific. In the recent High Court of Australia decision *Plaintiff M68/2015 v. Minister for Immigration and Border Protection* [2016] HCA 1 (3 February 2016) the Court held that an MOU signed between the Commonwealth of Australia and Nauru concerning the detention and offshore processing of "unauthorised maritime arrivals" was valid under § 61 of the Constitution. This means that the Australian government can continue to deport and detain children on Nauru, despite condemnation of this and the impact on children's mental and physical well-being.

137. Department of Immigration and Border Projection, Australian Government, *Immigration Detention and Community Statistics Summary (December 2015)* http://www.border.gov.au/about/reports-publications/research-statistics/statistics/live-in-australia/immigration-detention p. 9.

138. There are different categories of visas for people who are outside of Australia and are claiming refugee status based on persecution or substantial discrimination in their home country. People who are in Australia and have arrived without a valid visa may apply for a Temporary Protection visa or a Safe Haven Enterprise visa if the person intends to work or study in Australia: Department of Immigration and Border Projection, Australian Government, Refugee and Humanitarian Program http://www.border.gov.au/Trav/Refu.

139. Department of Education, Government of New South Wales, *Refugee Education* http://www.schools.nsw.edu.au/learning/yrk12focusareas/refugee/.

140. Refugee Council of Australia, *Education and Training*, http://unhcr.org.au/unhcr/images/convention%20and%20protocol.pdf.

141. RoadtoRefuge, *Refugees in Australia*, http://www.roads-to-refuge.com.au/refugees-australia/supporting-education.html.

142. Above note 140.

143. For example, the Victorian Department of Education supports a range of programs and services for students, families, and teachers, http://www.education.vic.gov.au/school/teachers/teachingresources/diversity/eal/pages/ealsupportrefugee.aspx. See also New South Wales education support programs for refugee children, http://www.schools.nsw.edu.au/learning/yrk12focusareas/refugee/.

Chapter Two

Malaysia

Fatt Hee Tie

INTRODUCTION

In Malaysia, both the government and private sector provide elementary and secondary education to all students. On the one hand, the federal government is responsible for delivering public elementary and secondary education in Malaysia by providing these schools with financial support along with employing their teachers.[1] On the other hand, private schools provide education to families that can afford to pay the tuition fees. Private organizations and companies have also established private schools. Students from families of a higher socioeconomic status are typically enrolled in the private schools. In addition, international schools offer both primary and secondary education to local children and students who are expatriates.

The general structure of the education system in the country is 6-3-3-2, namely: six years of primary education; three years of lower secondary education; two years of upper secondary education; and, two years of pre-university education. Students sit for a common public examination at the end of the third year of lower secondary education. Those who do well can choose to enter the science stream while the rest study in the social sciences or arts streams.

The duration is another two years of upper secondary education. At the end of upper secondary education, students can choose to continue for another two years of pre-university education in government schools. Some students select another option by enrolling in private colleges for the international examinations or pre-university foundation courses.

This chapter examines a variety of issues in education. After reviewing the legal and constitutional sources of education law in Malaysia, the chapter examines an array of issues addressing institutional issues, the rights of students and teachers, and emerging issues.

LEGAL AND CONSTITUTIONAL SOURCES OF EDUCATION LAW

Two primary pieces of legislation govern the Malaysian educational system, the Federal Constitution and the Education Act of 1996.[2] The Federal Constitution, the supreme law of Malaysia, provides the fundamental constitutional right to education for all children.[3]

According to Article 12(1) of the Federal Constitution, the right to education is as follows: there shall be no discrimination against any citizen on the grounds of religion, race, descent, or place of birth (a) in the administration of any educational institution maintained by a public authority, and, in particular, the admission of pupils or students or the payment of fees; or (b) in providing the funds of a public authority financial aid for the maintenance or education of pupils or students in any educational institution, regardless of whether they are maintained by a public authority and whether within or outside the federation.

The Federal Constitution also allows religious organizations to establish schools. Moreover, religious groups have the right to establish and maintain institutions for the education of children in its own religion without discrimination. The federal government and individual states of Malaysia establish, maintain, and assist Islamic institutions intended to provide instruction in the Islamic faith.[4]

The preamble to the Education Act of 1996 recognizes knowledge as the key factor determining the nation's destiny and survival.[5] This act expresses the purpose of education as being intended to equip Malaysians with the knowledge, skills, and values needed in a competitive global economy that is affected by rapid development in science, technology, and information. Another purpose of education identified in the act is to enable the country to attain the status of a fully developed nation in terms of economic development, social justice, and spiritual, moral, and ethical strength. Education is thus perceived as playing an important role in creating a united, democratic, liberal, and dynamic society. In this way, the education system seeks to realize the full potential of all individuals.

At the same time, the National Education Policy is based on the National Philosophy of Education. This policy strives to develop the potential of persons in a holistic and integrated manner so as to produce individuals who are intellectually, spiritually, emotionally, and physically balanced and harmonious, based on a firm belief in and devotion to God. Overall, the legal framework seeks to ensure that the education system achieve the purposes enunciated in both the Education Act 1996 and the National Philosophy of Education.

The Education Act of 1996 mandates Malay, as stipulated in Article 152 of the Federal Constitution,[6] the national language as the main medium of instruction in public schools. Additionally, there is a national curriculum and common examinations in public primary and secondary schools. The act's provisions encompass the following main areas: administration of the national education system; management of educational institutions; assessment and examinations; private educational institutions; registration of educational institutions, registration of teachers; and offenses and penalties.

In Malaysia, the Ministry of Education (MOE) often sends out administrative letters to officials in all public schools. These letters, known as administrative circulars, relate to such matters as guidelines and regulations on meting out corporal punishment in schools; sports activities; and procedures on suspension and expulsion of students. These administrative letters are valid and are binding on both public school teachers and students.

INSTITUTIONAL ISSUES

Elementary schools in Malaysia, commonly referred to as primary schools in the local context, and secondary schools are categorized into four types: national elementary schools,[7] national secondary schools,[8] national-type schools,[9] and private schools.[10]

The Education Act 1996 also promotes the establishment of private schools, defined as schools or educational institutions which are not government or government-aided schools or government educational institutions.[11] It is mandatory for all private schools to comply with the Education Act 1996. The Minister of Education can set out the regulations to supervise, regulate, or control the quality of education in private schools.

Compulsory Attendance in Elementary Schools

The duration of elementary education is six years. National or public schools, national-type schools, or private schools established under the Education Act of 1996 must provide courses of elementary education design for the duration of six years. However, elementary schooling may be completed within five to seven years.[12] Students who excel in the public examinations can complete their elementary educations in five years. Conversely, students who are weak in their studies can be retained in elementary schools for an extra school year.

Elementary education is compulsory in Malaysia. All parents who are Malaysian citizens residing in the country must ensure that if their children attained the age of six years on the first day of January of a current school year, they must be enrolled in an elementary school in that year and remain as pupils for the duration of the compulsory education.[13] Compulsory attendance laws only apply at the elementary level. Even so, the MOE may, if it considers it desirable and in the interest of pupils or the public to do so, can, by order published in the *Gazette*, exempt individual children or classes of students from having to attend compulsory education, either absolutely or subject to such conditions as it may deem fit to impose. Further, the MOE may, at any time, in its discretion, revoke, alter, or add to conditions to the exemption.

Parents who contravene the provision of ensuring their children attend elementary school can be punished. Parents who commit an offense can, on conviction, be made to pay a fine not exceeding five thousand ringgit or to imprisonment for a term not exceeding six months or both.[14]

Funding

Malaysia's education system is centralized with the federal government determining the policies and all matters related to educational finance. Each year, the federal government provides funds, via the MOE, to all public schools. The government sets aside part of the federal national budget during the national budget announcement in October each year to the MOE for education expenditure. Both public elementary and secondary schools received their funds from the government on an annual basis.

The federal government also provides capital grants to all public schools, payments from public funds to schools to construct new buildings, alter or extend existing facilities, or to purchase furniture or equipment. Conversely, private schools are self-financing, depending on the fees parents pay to cover the salaries of their staffs and all other expenses. The federal government does not provide any financial assistance to private schools.

Curriculum

Public elementary and secondary schools must teach the National Curriculum.[15] This curriculum specifies the knowledge, skills, and values that are expected to be acquired by pupils at the end of their respective periods of schooling. Further, the National Curriculum sets out the core subjects for all schools. Private elementary and secondary schools must also comply with the requirements of the National Curriculum; they must teach the core subjects and prepare students to sit for the common public examinations.[16]

Examinations

Educators in public elementary and secondary schools must prepare their students for the public school examinations. There are common public examinations for both elementary and secondary schools; the same public examination apply to private elementary and secondary schools.[17] Educators in private schools prepare students to sit for the international qualification examinations such as the International Baccalaureate (IB) and the Cambridge's International General Certificate of Secondary Education (IGCSE) examination. Students from families with higher incomes usually enroll and sit for these international examinations with the intention of furthering their studies at overseas universities.

Fees

Parents of public school students pay a nominal sum of money at the beginning of each new school year to be used for the Parent-Teachers' Association and other miscellaneous expenditure such as cocurricular activities. On the other hand, private school students pay both annual fees and monthly school fees, sums which can be relatively high.

School Uniforms

Rules in public elementary and secondary schools require students to wear standard school uniforms. Public elementary school students wear uniforms that are similar in color and design, usually consisting of white shirts and dark green trousers. Students in private schools also wear standard uniforms determined by officials at their institutions.

Boards of Governors

Malaysian law requires all schools, whether private or national[18] type schools, to create boards of governance to manage their activities. These boards set out the constitutions, boards of governors, and their chairs.

Private schools are required to comply with an additional set of rules and regulations because the Education Act of 1996 seeks to monitor them in a more stringent manner to ensure the quality of education. These provisions require private schools to establish boards of governors and to have their teachers register with the Registrar of Schools.[19]

The MOE is responsible for promulgating regulations overseeing boards of governors. These regulations may also regulate the management of the private school by a board of governors. Additional governors can be appointed if the ministry believes that discipline in schools is not adequately maintained; the terms of the instrument of government of a school are being willfully disregarded; or any provisions of the Education Act of 1996 or its accompanying regulations are being willfully disregarded.[20]

Boards of governors can be dissolved if they contravened provisions of the Education Act 1996 or its regulations, directions issued by the minister under section 9, or terms or conditions imposed under subsection 82(3). Boards can also be dissolved if they fail to observe or carry out provision of their instruments of governance, fail to prevent their schools from being used for purposes which are detrimental to the interests of the country or which are contrary to public interest, fail to prevent their institutions from being used for unlawful activities or purpose, or fail to prevent activities by unlawful organizations, societies, or other bodies of persons.[21]

If the MOE dissolves a board, it must specify in the notice the reasons for doing so and the date on which its order takes effect. Notices dissolving a board of governors may contain all such directions of incidental, consequential, ancillary, or transitional nature as the ministry deems necessary, expedient, or appropriate to provide. The minister can appoint a new board following the dissolution.[22]

Teacher Registration

Teachers in private schools must be registered in order to be allowed to teach.[23] Teachers in government or government-aided schools are not required to comply with this condition. Similarly, teacher trainees and those with permits to teach are exempted from this condition. The Registrar General of Schools maintains a register of all teachers.[24]

Registration of Private Schools

Private schools must register with the Registrar General of Schools which may impose terms and conditions deemed appropriate. Further, the Registrar General is responsible for keeping registry of private schools.[25]

Private Schools' Certificates of Registration

The Registrar General issues certificates of registration to the chairs of the boards of governors of private schools. These certificates must be exhibited in conspicuous locations in the private schools or educational institutions. Moreover, officials of the schools or institutions must comply with the conditions deemed appropriate by the Registrar General.[26]

The Registrar General can refuse to register private schools if they do not meet the prescribed standards of health and safety; they are used or likely to be used for purposes detrimental to the interests of the country, the public, or their pupils; the name under which they are to be registered is undesirable; existing private schools are already adequate in the area in which it is proposed to open the new private school; false or misleading statements are in materials concerning the applications for registration; the person applying for the registration fails or refuses to comply with the conditions imposed by the Registrar General; or the person appointed to as the chairman of the board of governors or head teacher is not a fit and proper or responsible individual to act in this capacity.[27]

If registration is denied, the Registrar General must send the notice of the refusal to officials of private schools together with specific reasons for doing so. Aggrieved applicants can appeal to the Minister of Education within twenty-one days of the notice being served. The decision of the minister is final. Private schools are not allowed to advertise until they have been registered or have been issued a provisional certificate of registration.[28]

The Registrar General can serve notice of intent to cancel a school's registration to the chairman of a board of governors or any person responsible for the management of the private school for the grounds: school discipline not being adequately maintained; the registration was obtained by reason of mistake or a false or misleading statement; the chairman of the board or other person responsible for a school's management made a false or misleading statement in a material promoting the school; there has been a breach of a term or condition imposed by the Registrar General; there is no chairman of the board of governors of the private school, or the person appointed to the position or as head teacher is not fit and proper or a responsible individual to act in such a capacity.[29]

Officials in schools that have received notice of the intended cancellation of their registrations have twenty-one days to file appeals with the MOE. If officials do not appeal or an appeal is rejected, the Registrar General may cancel the registration of the private school. Within twenty-one days of the cancellation, the chairman of the board of governors or other person responsible for the management of the private school must surrender its certificate of registration and its instrument of government to the Registrar General along with the individual certificates of registration for board members and teachers.[30]

As noted, all employees and governors of private schools must apply to the Registrar General to obtain a certificate of registration. Applications for registration may be refused if individuals were convicted of offenses by courts of law and sentenced to imprisonment for terms of not less than one year or a fine of no less than two thousand ringgit; otherwise than by reason only of a private school's having ceased to exist, been struck off a register established under the Education Act, or under the provisions of a previous corresponding written law; made a false or misleading statement in, or in connection with, an application for registration, or has intentionally suppressed a fact which is material to the application; or the applicant is not a citizen of Malaysia. The Registrar General can also refuse to register a person who is under the age of eighteen a governor of a private school.[31]

Refusals to register must be sent to applicant which may appeal to the Minister of Education within twenty-one days. The Registrar General has the power to strike off the register a governor or employee of a private school if such an individual obtained registration in consequence of a mistake or a false or misleading fact furnished in connection with an application for registration.[32]

Safety and Liability Issues

There is an increase in concern among parents and educational authorities over student safety. In fact, school activities impacting students have resulted in accidental death due to drowning,[33] serious physical injuries leading to blindness,[34] a broken arm,[35] and severe head injuries.[36] The standard of care and degrees of supervision is much higher in the elementary schools than secondary schools due to various factors such as the age, level of maturity, and experience of the students.

Tort liability covers two areas, intentional and unintentional torts. *Intentional torts* are deliberate acts committed by teachers with the intent of causing physical injuries to students. These acts include, for example, assault by pointing a cane to threaten a student; battery for slapping a student or excessive caning; false imprisonment such as class detention in an unlawful manner for an unreasonable period of time; and defamation, such as labeling students with derogatory terms. These acts contravene the provisions of the Penal Code in Malaysia.[37] On the other hand, an *unintentional tort* is a civil wrong committed when teachers fails to protect students from unreasonable risks of physical harm. The law of tort applies to both elementary and secondary schools.

Plaintiff parents can succeed in claims for negligence against the schools and teachers if they can prove the four elements in negligence. First, teachers owe students a duty of care to protect them from physical harm. Similarly, teachers can be liable because they assume the role of careful parents who take precautionary safety measures in reasonable manners to protect students from foreseeable harms. The doctrine of in loco parentis,[38] in the place of the parent, is also applicable in this context, particularly with regard to younger pupils.

Second, teacher breach the duty of care when they fail to provide appropriate standards of care because they have a legal duty to provide a reasonable amount of supervision to students. However, educators are not necessarily expected to provide constant supervision, particularly outside of school hours.[39]

In most of the judicial actions, parents alleged that teachers breached their duty of care by failing to provide adequate supervision in classes. In a dispute over supervision in a classroom, the court decided that the teacher did not carelessly expose the student to the type of injury that could have reasonably been foreseen.[40] The court explained that the evidence showed that the teacher provided adequate supervision and did not breach the duty of care.

In like manner, teachers are required to provide clear and proper instruction especially in situations where students faces higher risks of injury. In a case about supervision during a practical agriculture class, the court held that the teacher was negligent because she did not take reasonable and proper steps to prevent a student from getting injured.[41] Earlier, as the court pointed out, the MOE issued a letter to officials in all schools to remind teachers to take extra safety precautions with regard to the use of agricultural implements, laying down a set of mandatory safety guidelines to protect students from the risks of injuries.[42]

Third, a teacher's negligent conduct must cause an injury. For example, where a student from an elementary school drowned in an accident during a school picnic, her parents claimed that the teacher was negligent in failing to provide adequate supervision while she was playing a ball game in knee-deep water. The court rejected the allegation, ruling that the teacher provided a reasonable degree of supervision to ensure the student's safety of the students, adding that the evidence demonstrated that the teacher's conduct did not cause the harm.[43]

Fourth, pupils must have suffered physical injuries as a result of teachers' breaches of duty. In most cases, the plaintiff can prove this element successfully while the defendants have few defenses available such as contributory negligence and the voluntary assumption of risk. If both parties are found to be contributorily negligent, damages are apportioned based on the respective percentage of fault.[44]

TEACHER RIGHTS

Due Process

Public school teachers have the Federal Constitutional right to be treated impartially. The Constitution further guarantees that all public school teachers, irrespective of their race and/or grades in the profession, subject to the terms and conditions of their employment, must be treated in an impartial manner.[45]

The MOE is wholly responsible in determining the number of teachers needed in public schools by relying on long-term planning of the supply and demand of teachers. Both the faculty of education in public universities and teacher education institutes conduct teacher education programs to fulfill the needs of elementary and secondary public schools. Teacher trainees usually pursue four-year teacher education programs to obtain undergraduate degrees in education.

In some instances, those who already obtained undergraduate degrees in fields other than education may pursue one-year postgraduate diplomas in education to qualify as teachers. In the process, the MOE collaborates closely with the education faculties and teacher education institutes to ensure an adequate supply of teachers.

The MOE usually hires persons who completed teacher education programs. After a probationary period of between one and three years, teachers are placed in the permanent scheme of service or tenure. Teaches continue to teach until they reach the mandatory retirement age of sixty.[46]

The time-based system is used in the promotion of teachers. Following satisfactory service and based on the recommendations of their principals, teachers are promoted based on seniority. In schools, the scheme of promotion is from that of an ordinary teacher to one as a senior teacher, specialist teacher, senior school assistant, and finally, as a principal.[47]

There is security of tenure among public school teachers in most cases insofar as dismissal is rare. Almost all teachers serve in the public schools until the mandatory retirement age of sixty.[48] There are a few cases, though, of dismissal when teachers are convicted of crimes such as the criminal breach of trust and sexual offenses.

Teachers cannot be dismissed or reduced in rank by an authority of subordinate or lower rank. Only a committee with members whose ranks or positions are above that of the teacher can hear cases and make dismissals decisions.[49] Further, such mandatory procedures must comply with provisions in the Federal Constitution.[50]

The dismissal of teachers or having their ranks reduced without a reasonable opportunity of being heard is ultra vires. However, the opportunity to be heard is not accorded in three circumstances. First, a hearing is unnecessary if a criminal charge has been proved against a teacher. Second, there is no right to a hearing where the authority empowered to dismiss or reduce a teacher's rank is satisfied that for some reason, that must be recorded in writing because it was not reasonably practicable to carry out the requirements of this principle of natural justice. Third, a hearing is not required if a teacher's dismissal is in the interests of national security.[51]

In *Tan Tek Seng v. Suruhanjaya Perkhidmatan Pendidikan & Anor*,[52] the court examined the principle of natural justice and the constitutional rights of a teacher who was dismissed for refusing to return money belonging to another school employee. The trial proceedings and appeal went through four courts, the Sessions Court of Muar, the High Court of Muar, the High Court of Johor Bahru, and the Court of Appeal. The plaintiff, a senior assistant of an elementary school, was adjudged guilty and convicted by the Sessions Court of Muar for criminal breach of trust. The court then imposed a six-month imprisonment. On appeal, the High Court of Muar affirmed but set aside the punishment. Instead, the court directed the teacher to be of good behavior. Eventually, the Education Service Commission decided to dismiss the teacher.

On appeal, the High Court of Johor Bahru upheld the dismissal. Subsequently, the plaintiff appealed to the Court of Appeal which ordered a less severe punishment, namely, to reduce his rank to that of an ordinary teacher. Subsequently, the Court of Appeal reinstated the teacher on the ground that dismissal was disproportionate to the misconduct, explaining that the punishment was harsh, unfair, and unjust in view of the facts of the case.[53]

Freedom of Speech

The Federal Constitution provides for the right to freedom of speech, assembly, and association.[54] Accordingly, elementary and secondary school teachers have the rights to freedom of speech and expression, to assemble peacefully and without arms, and to form associations. Nevertheless, these rights are not absolute.

Malaysia's Parliament may, by law, impose restrictions on these rights if doing so is necessary in the interest of national security, public order, or morality. The restrictions are also designed to protect the privileges of Parliament and the Legislative Assembly as well as to protect against contempt of court, defamation, or incitement to any offense.

If speech interferes with or disrupts the teaching and learning process in schools, it can be prohibited. In a multiethnic and multicultural Malaysian society, the right to freedom of speech is further restricted to prohibit words and languages intended to incite racial hatred and/or to create disunity. In this context, the public interest outweighs the personal interests of individuals.

Freedom of Religion

Teachers in public and private schools have the right to profess and practice their religion and, subject to certain conditions, to propagate their faiths.[55] However, state law and federal law can control or restrict the propagation of any religious doctrine or belief among persons professing the religion of Islam. Teachers are restricted from propagating their religious beliefs and practices while in classrooms in order to prevent students, who are at impressionable ages, from being easily influenced by their teachers, who are considered to be role models.

Freedom of Association

Public school teachers have the freedom to become a member of the national teachers' union. However, the Public Officers (Conduct and Discipline) Regulations 1993 prohibit public school teachers from participation in politics. The Education Service Commission usually dismisses teachers who deliberately flouted the prohibition. This regulation does not apply to private school teachers.

Education Service Commission

Insofar as public school teachers and principals are deemed to be civil or public servants within the definition in the Federal Constitution,[56] the Malaysian government established an Education Service Commission (ESC) to recruit public school teachers, promote them, and manage their activities in the public service.[57] In addition, the ECC is also responsible for setting up disciplinary committees to hear cases of teacher misconduct. The government administrative regulations, also known as the Public Officers (Conduct and Discipline) Regulations of 1993, regulate the conduct and discipline of public school teachers.

On the other hand, the terms and conditions in their contracts govern the conduct of teachers in private schools. Further, the Employment Act plays an important role when teachers in private schools are dismissed, with the human resource department in these institutions obligated to comply with the principles of natural justice before acting.

STUDENT RIGHTS

Registration

It is the norm that many parents prefer to enroll their children in elementary and secondary schools demonstrating excellent academic results in the public examination. Schools with excellent academic results in the public examinations are also known as "elite" and "controled" public schools. These schools tend to have good discipline and are reputable. While many parents wish to enroll their children in these schools, the number of applications far exceeds the places available. As such, these "elite" schools have established their own individual entrance tests to select students for admission. To a certain extent, then, there is limited parental choice of schools, especially when places in the "elite" schools are very limited.

Generally, students are allowed to enroll in schools located near to their homes. However, some schools have been upgraded to the status of cluster schools of excellence. The MOE provides autonomy to officials in these schools to select their own students based on their own selection criteria. The selection criteria into secondary cluster schools focuses on good examination results at the elementary school level and active participation in cocurricular activities.

Consequently, students who reside near cluster schools may not be able to enroll in them if they fail to meet the criteria of the cluster schools. The upshot is that these parents do not have a choice to select a school near their place of residence and their children may have to travel to another school a distance away from their homes.

Private independent schools do not receive financial support from the government. Instead, officials in these schools collect fees from the pupils. Even so, the admissions process to these schools is highly competitive because parents believe that these schools provide better quality education, have better motivated teachers, better records of school discipline, and students there achieve better examination results.

An important feature of private schools is that they prepare students to sit for international tests such as the International Baccalaureate examination and the International General Certificate of Secondary Education examination. The Chinese Independent High Schools prepare their students for the Unified Examination Certificate (UEC). Private students studying for the Unified Examination Certificate at the Senior Middle Level (UEC-SML) sit for examinations in mathematics, biology, chemistry, physics, bookkeeping, accounting, and commerce.

The medium of instruction is in Mandarin and English. The UEC-SML is recognized as a qualification for entrance into universities in the United Kingdom, the United States, Taiwan, Hong Kong, China, Singapore, Australia, and Canada. Further, most private colleges in Malaysia recognize the qualifications. However, the government in Malaysia does not recognize the examination for entry into public universities.

Some Chinese independent high schools teach both the national secondary school curriculum and the independent school curriculum. The Malay language is the medium of instruction for the former while the medium of instruction is Mandarin for the latter. Students sit for two examinations: the government public examination and the private UEC examination. Thus, students have opportunities to obtain government-recognized examination results. Still, students face tremendous stress studying concurrently for both of the secondary school curricula.

Discipline

Student misconduct in elementary schools is generally minor in nature. Examples of misbehavior in elementary schools include failure to complete homework, and talking in class when a teacher is teaching. At the secondary school, misconduct can be more serious, ranging from truancy, smoking, and even fights.

Corporal punishment or caning in secondary school is conducted for serious disciplinary infractions but is rare at the elementary level. The principal or his appointed representative such as the disciplinary is vested with the authority to cane students. Caning is prohibited for female students.

The courts seldom interfere with the decision of school officials who discipline students. It is important to note that due process is mandatory to ensure students receive a fair and impartial treatment. Due process is guaranteed under Article 5(1) of the Federal Constitution, stated as "no person shall be deprived of his life or liberty save in accordance to the law."

In one case, a school expelled a student for committing various types of misconduct on multiple occasions. The student alleged that the principal violated the principle of natural justice because he was only given a mere warning that he might probably be expelled. The court held that the principle of natural justice was not violated because the principal need not have conducted an elaborate inquiry before making the decision to expel. Further, the court observed that the school fell within the category where the principle mandating a right to a hearing could be applied in a general manner rather than as a mandatory elaborate hearing.[58]

Freedom of Religion, Speech, and Dress

Students do not have an absolute right to practice the religions of their choice until they attain the age of eighteen.[59] Parents or guardians have the right to determine their religion of their children until they turn eighteen.[60] Moreover, Malaysia has yet to ratify the provision related to religion in the United Nations Convention on the Rights of the Child.

At issue in *Meor Atiqulraman bin Ishak & Ors. v. Fatimah bte Sihi & Ors*[61] was the constitutional right of students to wear a headgear to school. The headmistress expelled three elementary students who refused to follow her advice not to wear headgear to school. The parents claimed that the school violated the Federal Constitution that allows freedom of religion and freedom to wear the religious headgear. The Federal Court held that the school regulations did not contravene the Federal Constitution.

Students with Disabilities

Courts often consider the "best interests" of students with disabilities in matters related to their educational needs. In one case, a dispute arose when school officials rejected a student's application to enroll due to a physical disability impacting his motor ability on the basis that creating a disability-friendly environment would have resulted in their incurring heavy expenses. The court held that the financial expenditure in making the school disabled friendly was not legally tenable, reiterating that students with disabilities have a basic right to education that overrides financial considerations.[62]

EMERGING ISSUES

As in many nations, student use of mobile or hand phones is an emerging issue as parents wish for their children to be allowed to bring phones to school so they can be reached in emergency situations. Yet the MOE forbids students from bringing phones to school because they can interfere with the teaching and learning environment.[63]

Another emerging issue is the increase in students' misconduct in elementary schools. Bullying in schools has increased despite measures adopted to keep schools safe. The severity of students' misconduct has also increased. In response, the MOE has established a standard operating procedure to enable school officials to respond to these concerns effectively.[64]

CONCLUSION

Malaysian laws and regulations have been effective in regulating the conduct of teachers and students in public and private elementary and secondary schools. Tenured teachers in public schools usually possess undergraduate qualification in teacher education from either the education faculties of the public universities or the public teachers' institutes. On the other hand, not all teachers in the private schools possess similar qualifications.

The demand for places in private schools has increased in recent years as well-to-do families often enroll their children in these schools based on the perception that they offer better teaching and learning environments. A more important reason for this increase may be that the medium of instruction in private schools is usually English. Even so, the law continues to play an important role in monitoring and maintaining the quality of education in private schools as well as in public schools in the face of new and emerging issues.

NOTES

1. See generally, http://www.moe.gov.my/en/home. The population of Malaysia is about 30 million. As of 31 December 2014, there are 7,760 public elementary schools and 2,394 public secondary schools in the country. The overall number of schools is 10,154. The number of students in elementary school is 2,704,046 and in secondary schools, 2,220,679. The overall total number of students is 5,120,802. There are 238,073 teachers in the elementary school and 181,747 teachers in the secondary school. The overall total number of teachers is 419,820.
2. The Education Act is available at http://www.ilo.org/dyn/natlex/docs/ELECTRONIC/95631/112655/F1187461074/MYS95631.pdf.
3. Article 4(1) of the Federal Constitution.
4. Article 12(2) of the Federal Constitution.
5. See note 2.
6. Ibid. Sections 2 and 17.
7. Under Section 2 of the Education Act 1996, "national school" means a government or government-aided primary school—(a) providing primary education appropriate for pupils from the age of six years; (b) using the national language as the main medium of instruction; (c) in which the English language is a compulsory subject of instruction; and (d) in which facilities for the teaching of— (i) the Chinese or Tamil language shall be made available if the parents of at least fifteen pupils in the school so request; and (ii) indigenous languages shall be made available if it is reasonable and practicable so to do and if the parents of at least fifteen pupils in the school so request.

8. Ibid. A "national secondary school" means a government or government aided secondary school—(a) providing a five-year course of secondary education appropriate for pupils who have just completed primary education; (b) using the national language as the main medium of instruction; (c) in which the English language is a compulsory subject of instruction; (d) in which facilities for the teaching of—(i) the Chinese or Tamil language shall be made available if the parents of at least fifteen pupils in the school so request; (ii) indigenous languages shall be made available if it is reasonable and practicable so to do and if the parents of at least fifteen pupils in the school so request; and (iii) Arabic, Japanese, German, or French or any other foreign language may be made available if it is reasonable and practicable so to do; and (e) preparing pupils for such examinations as may be prescribed, and includes any such school providing a transition class.

9. According to Section 2 of the Education Act 1996: "national-type school" means a government or government-aided primary school—(a) providing primary education appropriate for pupils from the age of six years; (b) using the Chinese or Tamil language as the main medium of instruction; and (c) in which the national and English languages are compulsory subjects of instruction.

10. Under Section 2 of the Education Act 1996: "private school" or "private educational institution" means a school or an educational institution which is not a government or government-aided school or educational institution.

11. Ibid.
12. Ibid. Section 29.
13. Ibid. Section 29(A).
14. Ibid. Section 22(4).
15. Ibid. Section 18.
16. Ibid. Section 74.
17. Ibid. Section 74.
18. Ibid. Section 87.
19. Ibid. Section 81 ff.
20. Ibid. Section 56.
21. Ibid. Section 59.
22. Ibid. Section 60.
23. Ibid. Section 103.
24. Ibid.
25. Ibid. Section 80.
26. Ibid. Section 82.
27. Ibid. Section 84.
28. Ibid. Section 85.
29. Ibid. Section 87.
30. Ibid. Section 87.
31. Ibid. Section 90.
32. Ibid. Sections 91–93.
33. *Chen Soon Lee v. Chong Voon Pin & Ors* [1966] 2 MLJ 264.
34. *Government of Malaysia & Ors v. Jumat bin Mahmud & Anor* [1977] 2 MLJ 103.
35. *Zazlin Zahira Hj Kamarulzaman & Anor v. Louis Marie Neube RT Ambrose a/l J Ambrose & Ors* [1994] 3 AMR 2518.
36. *Mohamed Raihan bin Ibrahim & Anor v. Government of Malaysia & Ors* [1981] 2 MLJ 27.
37. Penal Code (Act 574).
38. *Williams v. Eady* (1893) 10 TLR 4.
39. *Camkin v. Bishop* [1941] 2 All ER 713.
40. *Government of Malaysia & Ors v. Jumat bin Mahmud & Anor* [1977] 2 MLJ 103.
41. *Mohamed Raihan bin Ibrahim & Anor v. Government of Malaysia & Ors* [1981] 2 MLJ 27.
42. Ibid. at 27.
43. *Chen Soon Lee v. Chong Voon Pin & Ors* [1966] 2 MLJ 264.

44. *Headmistress, Methodist Girls School & Ors v Headmaster, Anglo-Chinese Primary School & Anor* [1984] 1 MLJ 293.
45. Article 136 Federal Constitution.
46. Available at: http://minretirementage.mohr.gov.my/.
47. Hazri Jamil, Nordin Abd. Razak, Reena Raju, and Abdul Rashid Mohamed, Teacher Professional Development in Malaysia: Issues and Challenges, available at http://aadcice.hiroshima-u.ac.jp/e/publications/sosho4_2-08.pdf.
48. Ibid.
49. Article 132 Federal Constitution.
50. Article 135 Federal Constitution.
51. Article 135 (2) Federal Constitution.
52. [1995] 2 AMR 1913, HC.
53. [1996] 2 AMR 1617; [1996] 1 MLJ 261, CA.
54. Article 10 Federal Constitution.
55. Article 11 Federal Constitution.
56. Article 132 Federal Constitution.
57. Article 141A Federal Constitution.
58. *Mahadevan v. Anandarajan & Ors*. [1970] 1 MLJ 50.
59. Article 12(4) Federal Constitution.
60. Ibid.
61. [2000] 1 AMR 366.
62. See generally, *Jakob Renner (an infant suing through his father and next friend, Gilbert Renner) & Ors. v. Scott King, Chairman of the Board of Directors of the International School of Kuala Lumpur & Ors.* [2000] 5 MLJ 254.
63. MOE, Malaysia, Professional Circular No.2/2009, *Enforcement of Prohibition of the Talking Handphone and Its Use among Students in School*, available at http://www.moe.gov.my/images/pekeliling/2009/circularfile_file_000297.pdf.
64. MOE, Malaysia, Professional Circular no. 8, 2011 Management of Students' Safety in School, available at: http://www.moe.gov.my/images/pekeliling/2011/circularfile_file_000926.pdf.

Chapter Three

New Zealand-Aotearoa

Sally Varnham[1]

INTRODUCTION

Historically, there has not been a discreet discipline known as "Education Law" in New Zealand.[2] The term more correctly refers to the wide body of policy, statutes, common law, and international instruments which comprise the right to education and rights in education. Recent decades have seen a greater recognition of the myriad of ways in which the law impacts on education along with the attendant and increasing need for scholarship and discourse between and among lawyers, law, and education practitioners and scholars.[3]

This chapter explores the law as it applies to the exercise of the right to, and the rights in, education by New Zealand children and young people. It begins by tracing the history and development of the "free, compulsory and secular" system of compulsory education. The chapter next considers the exercise by young people of particular rights within education which apply equally to educators, for example, the right not to be discriminated against. Then it touches on legislation and policy relating particularly to the employment of those educators. The chapter concludes by discussing some emerging issues faced by schools and educators while considering the challenges and opportunities presented by modern developments to the education system as a whole and impact on every child attending school in New Zealand.

Education is clearly the key to the realization of life's expectations and to the future of the nation. As such, the exercise of the right to education is fundamental to the welfare of society. While the implementation of successive government policies may often lead one to question the ideal, it is axiomatic that education is a public good. In New Zealand, it has been said that the rationale for this, since the beginnings of the education system, is contained in four key points: "Social control, the need for an educated electorate, investment in economic productivity, and equal individual rights."[4]

THE SOURCES OF EDUCATION LAW: THE HISTORICAL DEVELOPMENT OF COMPULSORY ATTENDANCE IN A BICULTURAL NATION

New Zealand is a constitutional monarchy with an "unwritten" constitution comprised of some statutes, common law, and constitutional conventions. While New Zealand was settled largely from Great Britain, it has always been bicultural, having a large indigenous Māori population.

In 1840, the Treaty of Waitangi was entered into between many, though not all, of the Māori chiefs and the British Crown that resulted in the declaration of British sovereignty over New Zealand.[5] Māori gave the crown an exclusive right to buy lands they wished to sell, and, in return, they were guaranteed full rights of ownership of their lands, forests, fisheries, and other possessions (their "taonga" or treasures), and they were given the rights and privileges of British subjects.[6]

It is important to note in this context that, while different understandings and recognition of the treaty[7] have led to much debate, litigation, and inquiry, it is now considered to be the founding document of New Zealand. While it is not considered to be domestic law, the treaty's principles are incorporated within all government legislative, executive, and judicial functions. This, of course, includes the public function of compulsory education and all that entails.

The Māori language or te Reo was, in 1986, held to be a treasure or "taonga"[8] and shortly afterward it became an official language. The Māori Language Commission was established to promote the use of Māori as a "living language" and "an ordinary means of communication."[9] This is strongly significant to any discussion of education in terms of biculturalism and the right to language and culture, manifested particularly in Māori language teaching and Māori immersion schooling.

Almost from the arrival of the first settlers, schools were established usually by churches and private enterprise for their children. However, until the 1870s there was no law requiring compulsory attendance and less than half of New Zealand children attended school. Prior to that time and pursuant to a policy of assimilation of Māori children, government subsidies were provided to missionaries to run schools in the English language for Māori children.[10] Consequently religion had a strong influence both on early schooling and on Māori culture, the latter which remains true to this day.

In 1877, the *Education Act* laid the foundations for the system of national state-funded and state-controlled system of education which exists today.

While education was compulsory for Pakeha (non-Māori) children, it did not become compulsory for Māori children until 1894. In 1903, provision was made for free places in secondary schools for children who completed their primary education.[11]

In 1944, secondary education was made free and compulsory until the age of fifteen. It is startling that while for some time Māori attended Education Board schools, it was not until 1969 that the Native or Māori schools system with its assimilationist policies ceased to exist. In following decades, and particularly since 1984, New Zealand law and society have seen increasing moves toward biculturalism with both an obligation and a national determination to incorporate a Māori dimension into all areas of public life.[12]

This is especially clear in education legislation. One example is that when school officials are formulating their charters, as required by the *Education Act 1989*, they must consult with the local Māori community. Further, all charters are deemed to contain a provision for schools to provide instruction in Māori language and culture where there is a call for doing so.[13]

In the late 1970s at the impetus of kaumatua or Māori elders, a call for education in the Māori language emerged and kōhanga reo or preschool Māori language nests were established to address the decline of te reo Māori (Māori language) and tikanga Māori (Māori culture, cultural habits, and practices). Now pursuant to the *Education Act 1989*, a system of education in the Māori language operates in tandem with English language schools; these schools, Kura Kaupapa now within Designated Character Schools, are state funded, state controlled, and compulsory in the same manner as all state schooling.

"Tomorrow's Schools": The Devolution of Education Administration

In the 1980s with the introduction of a government policy known as "Tomorrow's Schools," the provision of state education in New Zealand underwent major reforms embodied in the *Education Act 1989*.[14] The Department of Education was disbanded with schools becoming autonomous entities, managed by principals and governed by locally elected Boards of Trustees.[15]

Schooling during the compulsory years from six to sixteen is now provided in New Zealand by state-funded government schools; Partnership Schools Kura Hourua; Designated Character Schools (including Kura Kaupapa); partially state-funded, state-integrated schools; private and independent schools which also receive a level of state funding[16]; or Correspondence schools Te Aho o Te Kura Pounamu which will be transitioned into a new Community of Online Learning (COOL) by December 2018 (Part 3A). New entrants to the provision of compulsory government-funded schooling are Partnership Schools Kura Hourua, referred to as such in the newly amended

Education Act 1989[17] While New Zealand children traditionally began school attendance on their fifth birthdays, there is now provision for "cohort" transition from preschool (sections 5A–5C *Education Act 1989*). Attendance is now compulsory for children who are enrolled in school under six (section 25 *Education Act 1989*).

The Ministry of Education describes partnership schools as "a type of school in our education system, that bring together education, the business sector and community groups to provide new opportunities for students to achieve education success. Partnership Schools have greater freedom and flexibility to innovate and engage with their students in return for stronger accountability for improving educational outcomes."[18] These schools give as their rationale for existence a focus on the government's priority groups: Māori, Pasifika, learners from low socioeconomic backgrounds, and learners with special education needs. An authorization board advises the minister on the approval of new schools and on the educational performance of the schools, once established.

The establishment of these government-funded schools, which are, in many respects, outside of the constraints of state schools, has been extremely controversial.[19] It has been suggested that these schools may be set up by particular faiths and minority cultures and while there is, as yet, little evidence of this being realized, these schools are viewed by many with some skepticism. The legislation includes a responsibility for the "sponsor" to ensure a safe physical and emotional environment for students.

Although self-managed, all New Zealand schools must operate according to the National Education and Learning Priorities (to be issued following consultation) and the National Education Guidelines (NAGS) which are statements of goals, policy, curriculum, codes of administration, and so forth.[20] It is a strong focus of the new amendments to the *Education Act 1989* (contained in the *Education (Update) Amendment Act 2017*) that education providers at all levels work together to help all young people achieve their full potential. For this purpose the legislation provides for the growth of Communities of Learning: Kahui Ako which comprise schools, kura kaupapa, early learning and tertiary providers and their collaboration in sharing expertise in teaching and learning (sections 71C–75 *Education Act 1989*). The NAGS provide, among other things, that school officials must provide safe physical and emotional environments for students.[21] While the stated aim of "Tomorrow's Schools" was to allow "community responsive" schools, the institution of the NAGs and NEGS have arguably led to uniformity rather than diversity.[22]

A form of safeguard for "non-performing" schools is incorporated within the *Education Act 1989* by a framework for statutory interventions.[23] Where there are concerns about the operation of individual state and integrated schools, or relating to the welfare or educational performance, there are a number of different interventions which may be made by the Secretary of Education, from requiring information to dissolving a board of trustees and appointing a limited statutory manager or commissioner.[24]

THE RIGHT TO EDUCATION AND THE STATE'S RESPONSIBILITY

The *Education Act 1989* currently provides for free education for New Zealand children in state, state-integrated schools (sections 3 and 441), and correspondence schools (see above).

The onus of ensuring the exercise of the right to education entails, in the words of the late Katerina Tomaschevski, the United Nations Special Rapporteur on the Right the Education,[25] the provision of an education which is available to all without discrimination, with universal accessibility to education facilities, that is acceptable as far as possibility to all children and their parents, and which includes its adaptability to the needs of individual students. Within the New Zealand context this has been aptly and succinctly described as a state responsibility to ensure a system of education which is "regular, systemic and [,] not unsuitable."[26]

This philosophy is contained in the 1939 much-quoted words by the then Labour Prime Minister, the Hon Peter Frazer:

> The government's objective, broadly expressed, is that every person, whatever his [their] level of ability, whether he [they are] is rich or poor, whether he [they] lives in town or country, has a right, as a citizen to a free education of the kind for which he is [they are] best suited and to the fullest extent of their powers.[27]

These words have underpinned the nature of New Zealand schooling since its first national inception[28] and it is often said that the principles of egalitarianism and racial harmony were and continue today to be the cornerstones of New Zealand compulsory education. While essentially a strong belief that these ideals[29] continues to be the theoretical thread running through education today, there are modern circumstances which make it perhaps questionable whether in reality rather than rhetoric they have survived the various policy and statutory provisions which govern its provision.

School Boards of Trustees may put in place enrollment schemes for schools, pursuant to the *Education Act 1989* by which they may set school zones and make provisions (also provided in the act) for access to the school for children who are out of designated zones. These provisions must have as their overriding purpose the prevention of overcrowding while ensuring access to all children within school zones.[30] As elsewhere, because New Zealand schools strive to attract international students, the act provides for the enrollment and charging of fees to international students in particular schools (section 4).

Education for Children with Special Needs

New Zealand is a signatory to the International Convention on the Rights of Persons with Disabilities. Its education system is built around the principle of "[F]ull and effective participation and inclusion in society" (Article 3(c)) and specifically the philosophy of inclusion in education [Article 24]). This is also in keeping with state obligations under Article 23.1 of the United National Convention on the Rights of the Child.

A policy of equal opportunity in education is by way of "mainstreaming" provided for in the *Education Act 1989*, Section 8:

> Equal rights to primary and secondary education(1) Except as provided in this Part, people who have special educational needs (whether because of disability or otherwise) have the same rights to enrol and receive education at State schools as people who do not.[31]

This legislation led to the introduction in 2000 of a government scheme known as Special Education 2000 (SE2000).[32] The policy of equality of access aimed to abolish most special schools and facilities, replacing them with funding to all schools, within a prescribed resourcing system to accommodate children according to their disabilities. The policy did not suit everyone.

Daniels v. the Attorney-General[33] was a challenge by way of judicial review of the minister's decision leading to SE2000 by a group of parents of children with special needs. They contended that the policy amounted to a breach of the rights of their children to education, which, they argued, was best fulfilled in special education facilities. J. Baragwanath of the High Court agreed.

The Court of Appeal, while adopting this view in principle, overturned the decision that the minister's policy could be challenged by individuals. The judges held that the right to education as provided in the act was a public statutory right to be educated in a system designed to ensure regularity and quality, and to which there was universal access. This, they said, was provided by SE2000. It followed that it was not a right which was enforceable by individual students. However, the judges did accept, that there were specified rights of children which could be enforced within the education context such as due process in school exclusion and equal opportunity rights.[34]

The implementation of SE2000 remains controversial, particularly in considering the discipline of children with special needs for behavior often caused by or related to their disabilities; this is discussed below in the section on school discipline for *A v. Hutchinson*[35] and the new government inquiry.[36]

Despite the reservations, it is heartening to note that the Education Review Office (ERO) concluded from its evaluation of inclusive practices in 152 schools (reviewed in Term 2, 2014) that: "Three quarters of the schools were mostly inclusive of students with special needs, compared with only half in ERO's 2010 evaluation."[37]

THE RIGHT TO EDUCATION IN A SAFE ENVIRONMENT

Physical safety

As discussed above, all schools in New Zealand are autonomous and are controlled and managed individually by boards of trustees. These boards have a mandated responsibility to provide safe physical and emotional environments for students.[38]

In addition, legislative responsibility for safety is now contained in three new statutes. There is an overriding health and safety statute which imposes duties and obligations on officials in schools because they are within the definition of entities conducting a "business or undertaking."

The new *Health and Safety at Work Act 2015*, together with other associated regulations and statutes, imposes strict duties on school boards of trustees to eliminate risk, as far as is reasonably practicable, or minimize if not practicable. The act imposes criminal sanctions for breach on boards but not on individual members. Under the act, it is not possible contracted out of the primary duty[39] and it covers the health and safety of workers, teachers and all school staff, and all who come to schools such as students, voluntary workers, and parents.

Other legislative duties relating to safety are also imposed by *Vulnerable Children Act 2014*, which requires all school authorities to have child protection policies in place, including safety checks on all who regularly associate with children in the schools, whether paid staff or volunteers; the *Food Act 2014* which relates to food safety in businesses generally and applies to food being sold in schools; and the provisions in section 71A *Education Act 1989* relating to off-site education.

In terms of civil liability, since 1974 it has not been possible in New Zealand to sue for compensatory damages for personal injury by accident. The right to sue in negligence was surrendered by New Zealanders following the enactment of the first *Accident Compensation Act 1972*, in what was known as a "social contract" (referred to as ACC). The no-fault, comprehensive system of compensation for personal injury by accident is now embodied in the *Accident Compensation Act 2001*.[40] This act eliminates the potential for school liability in negligence which faces schools and education departments in comparative jurisdictions. While the scheme has a strong focus on injury prevention and rehabilitation, it provides for a system of earnings related compensation, which applies to all school employees while providing lump sum entitlements for permanent impairment.

It is not possible within the confines of this chapter to discuss the provisions of the ACC system,[41] except to note that since 2005[42] it has covered mental injury suffered as a result of sexual abuse (extending to that relating to abuse which took place before 1974 when ACC came into force). Within the context of teachers and other school staff, it now also covers mental injury resulting from witnessing severe traumatic events at work.[43]

Bullying and Harassment

Bullying in schools and now the prevalence of cyberbullying is a perennial issue receiving increasing attention. Bullying threatens the safety of children both inside and outside of school environments and is now recognized as a human rights issue. Yet effective, long-term responses continue to challenge educators, policy makers, and legislators alike. All forms of bullying are now recognized as a precipitating factor for truancy or lack of engagement of children in their education.

Bullying's effects are both short-term, in preventing education in safe atmospheres conducive to learning, and long-term in being causative of psychiatric and emotional harm, even leading to suicide. Research shows it to be a factor which may lead parents to homeschool their children with disabilities.[44]

Clearly, school environments in which bullying is allowed to exist are counterproductive to the exercise of the right to education, for the "victims," the "bullies," and for whole school communities. A Bullying Prevention Advisory Group has been constituted to provide a wide-ranging national response, its comprehensive membership comprising representatives from all education sectors and stakeholders as well as the Commissioner for Children, the Ministries of Social Development and Justice, Netsafe, and the New Zealand Police. The extensive work of this body has culminated in a comprehensive "Bullying Prevention and Response: A Guide for Schools."[45] This work runs in tandem with a strong focus of schools on the building of school cultures with healthy, respectful, and responsible social interactions where bullying has no place.

New Zealand is no different than other nations in that the complexity in issues relating to cyberbullying and the misuse of social media poses many new challenges for school officials. These challenges are discussed at the conclusion of this chapter.

SECULAR EDUCATION—FREEDOM OF RELIGION AND FREEDOM FROM RELIGION

In addition to Māori, New Zealand now has an increasingly diverse multicultural and multiethnic population. This is due in no small part to the large and increasing population of Polynesians and other Pacific Islanders, as well as the immigration and resettlement of people, refugees, and asylum seekers. Secularism, and the rights and freedoms associated with religious belief, give rise to complex issues in public education. Questions arise generally in two respects—both in connection with freedom of religion, and freedom from religion.

Unlike its close neighbor Australia, New Zealand does not have a constitutional separation of church and state so it is saved from the issues faced there by state funding of denominational schools and other religious affiliated processes.[46] It is true to say that the state system of education historically, as established by the *Education Act 1877*, is secular in nature.[47] Yet the reality is that in the years since the enactment of the *Private Schools Conditional Integration Act 1975* (PSCIA) (now incorporated within the *Education Act 1989*), schools with religious affiliations in New Zealand, predominantly those established by the Catholic Church but also Protestant churches in the early days of New Zealand's nationhood, now receive a large measure of government funding.

These state-integrated schools provide education of a "special character" meaning "education within the framework of a particular or general religious or philosophical belief and associated with observances and traditions appropriate to that belief."[48]

Pursuant to the PSCIA, these schools enter into integration agreements with the crown whereby they retain ownership of their property, required to be brought up to the standard of public school facilities at the proprietor's cost but then maintained by the state. They are authorized to charge "attendance dues" for this purpose, clarified in *New Zealand Catholic Education Office Limited v. Attorney-General*.[49] Staff salaries are paid by the state.

The incorporation of religion within government schools inevitably raises many complex issues relating to religious freedom, arising in no small extent from the changed nature of New Zealand society since the drafting of the current provisions relating to religious instruction in schools in 1964.[50] It provides that public schools may have religious observances and may provide religious education as part of broader contexts, rather than instruction in particular religions.[51]

The secular nature of public education in New Zealand is accepted to mean "nonsectarian," allowing for schools to provide general religious instruction or nondenominational education to students.[52] In additions, schools may provide special religious instruction if there is demonstrated sufficient demand in school communities, and parents may request that their children "opt out" of religious education classes.

Government censuses now reveal a dramatic increase in New Zealanders who declare themselves to be of "no religion."[53] It has been said that there is a "trend now towards new generations of secular New Zealanders questioning long standing laws and practices in education such as schools producing religious pageants."[54] Also, New Zealand society has become considerably more ethnically and culturally diverse.

School boards of trustees have considerable discretion as to what they provide in terms of religious instruction or observances but this must be done within guidelines, particularly the ability to opt out[55] and in a nondiscriminatory way.[56] Religious education must be in accordance with human rights protections under the *NZBORA*, to freedom of thought, conscience, and religion (section 13), the right to manifest religion or belief (section 15), freedom from discrimination (section 19), and the rights of minorities not to be denied the right to enjoy their culture, practice, religion, or language (section 20).

It is common for schools to have practices such as *karakia*[57] and *tikanga* Māori which often contain strong religious overtones.[58] This frequently presents a tension for schools between the strong commitment to biculturalism in New Zealand society and freedom from religion.

Finally, related issues of freedom of religion are connected with freedom of expression and the exercise of rights and freedoms connected to religious manifestation and expression, inevitable in our new diverse societies. Insofar as the freedoms of thought, conscience, and religion, contained in section 13 NZBORA, extends to the right of pupils to wear items such as headscarves, kirpans, crucifixes, *taonga*, and the like, school officials are required to justify any restriction they impose in this regard.

The HRA provides a mechanism for resolution of complaints through mediation, administered by the New Zealand Human Rights Commission with its provisions having been invoked on many occasions in the education context.[59] It is true now that the reality of New Zealand's multicultural, multiethnic, and multireligious society calls for a revisiting of policies relating to religion in public schools, and in public life generally.

RIGHTS IN EDUCATION

New Zealand has a robust rights culture, manifested formally in its ratification of international conventions such as the Universal Declaration of Human Rights, the International Covenant on Economic, Social and Cultural Rights, the Universal Covenant on Civil and Political Rights, the Convention on the Rights of Persons with Disabilities, and the United Nations Convention on the Rights of the Child (UNCROC), along with its incorporation of the principles within these instruments in domestic legislation.

A strong role is played by the principles of the Treaty of Waitangi te tiriti o Waitangi and the *New Zealand Bill of Rights Act 1990* (NZBORA).[60] This act affirms, protects, and promotes human rights and fundamental freedoms in respect of public office and public functions, including the right to natural justice, nondiscrimination, bodily integrity, those of minorities to language and culture and so forth. It expressly includes, among other rights, the rights to freedom of thought, conscience, and religion (section 13), freedom of expression (section 14), and to be secure from unreasonable search and seizure (section 21).

The rights in NZBORA clearly apply to the actions of state schools in respect of students and staff alike. Further, it has been strongly argued that these rights apply to the actions of private schools insofar as they are performing the public function of education, albeit privately.[61] In any event, in the context of private interaction, the *Human Rights Act 1993* (HRA) provides protections for equal opportunity and antidiscrimination in all areas of private and public life.

Anti-discrimination

Discrimination on any grounds by an educational establishment is prohibited under section 57 of the *Human Rights Act 1993*:

1. It shall be unlawful for an educational establishment, or the authority responsible for the control of an educational establishment, or any person concerned in the management of an educational establishment or in teaching at an educational establishment,—

    a. to refuse or fail to admit a person as a pupil or student; or
    b. to admit a person as a pupil or a student on less favorable terms and conditions than would otherwise be made available; or
    c. to deny or restrict access to any benefits or services provided by the establishment; or
    d. to exclude a person as a pupil or a student or subject him or her to any other detriment,—

    by reason of any of the prohibited grounds of discrimination.

These prohibited grounds are set out in section 21 of that act and the matters contained there with most relevance to education are religious or ethical belief, sex and sexual orientation, color, race, ethnic or national origins. In terms of disability, discrimination is a breach of section 21(1) (h) of the act. These provisions are also incorporated within the NZBORA, section 19 of which was referred to above.[62]

Within the HRA "disability" is widely defined to include physical disability or impairment, physical or psychiatric illness, intellectual or psychological disability or impairment, any other loss or abnormality of psychological, physiological, or anatomical structure or function, reliance on a guide dog, wheelchair, or other remedial means, or the presence in the body of organisms capable of causing illness; this section should be read in conjunction with the previous account of provision for special needs education.

Complaints are commonly made to the Human Rights Commission (HRC) and settled there. However, a matter may reach the courts within the context of school discipline, framed as an Application for Judicial Review of a decision to suspend a child with special needs, discussed below.[63] Issues relating to disability and education are an ongoing concern, particularly because schools are faced with increasing numbers of children with behavioral difficulties which may from time to time threaten school safety and limited resources.

The HRC reports that it received major complaints from national disability organizations which cite systemic discrimination against disabled students within education policies and practices" and that "[T]he breadth and details of these complaints . . . highlighted the barriers that disabled children and young people and their families face"[64] in exercising their right to education.

The HRC stated that in the years since 2002, over half of the complaints and enquiries it received in this area related to four general themes: problems surrounding the enrollment of children in schools, exclusions from schools because of their disabilities or for behavior caused by their disabilities, funding of support and assistance, and the ability of children with disabilities to participate in wider activities such as school camps.

The HRC concluded that there are significant outstanding issues relating to all four of the "A" components: accessibility—participation rates are disproportionately low; availability—an insufficient number of people are trained as special needs educators; acceptability—education standards vary for students with a disability as to those without; and adaptability—provision does not reasonably accommodate the needs for the education of children with special needs.

The HRC noted that the International Convention on the Rights of Persons with Disabilities acknowledged the complexities of inclusive education, and the need to provide effective individual support to maximize development, "by focusing on educational outcomes, rather than the educational setting alone."[65] There had been similar shortcomings reported earlier, in the HRC 2004 report *Human Rights in New Zealand Today Nga Tika*

Tangata o te motu and its *2005–2010 Action Plan for Human Rights: Mana ki te Tangata*.

These reports raised major national concern about barriers to the right to education of children with disabilities which led the government to set up a Review of Special Education 2010 (the Review). It aimed at conducting a wide examination of the lack of services in terms of nature and extent provided since the inception of Special Education 2000. The Review gathered wide opinion from across the sector, including parents and *whānau*, "to identify the need for increasing inclusive practices in schools, raising achievement for learners with special education needs/disabilities, and reducing bureaucracy and making special education services (provided by the Ministry and schools) easier for parents and *whānau*[66] to access and navigate."

The Review was heralded as representing a turning point in special education, but there is very little evidence of change. In 2015, the government set up an "Inquiry into the identification and support for students with the significant challenges of dyslexia, dyspraxia and autism spectrum disorders in primary and secondary schools."[67] The call for submissions ended in October 2015 and the report was presented to the New Zealand Parliament in November 2016. The New Zealand government responded in February 2017.[68]

SCHOOL DISCIPLINE: EXCLUSIONARY MEASURES

Exclusion from school has severe impact on the exercise of students' right to education. Research shows that even short-term suspensions disengage children from schooling, with many often failing to return. Very often it sets young persons on a path of offending, in the US termed "the schoolyard to jail yard track." Sadly, the numbers of New Zealand children excluded from school by disciplinary action is high and rising, with an overrepresentation of students who are Pacific Islanders and Māori.[69]

Sections 13–18 of the *Education Act 1989* set out the framework and the Education (Stand-down, Suspension, Exclusion, and Expulsion) Rules 1999 provide the operational detail for a range of measures for school exclusion as disciplinary measures from state schools.[70] However, it is a stated intention that these measures be considered within the "broader philosophy of education" as set out in the Act and in the National Education Guidelines[71] which embody the right to education, an obligation on school boards of trustees to help all students to realize their full potential and address individual and cultural barriers to learning, obligations on principals to ensure good guidance and counseling for all students, and to ensure all reasonable steps are taken to ensure parents are told of matters which are impeding students' learning (section 77 *Education Act 1989*).

Section 13 of the *Education Act 1989* clearly highlights the centrality of minimizing disruption to students' school attendance while ensuring adherence to natural justice. A high standard is required by Section 14 which provides for a range of disciplinary responses entailing school exclusion: stand-down for a short period, suspension, and expulsion. A principal must be satisfied on reasonable grounds that:

a. The student's gross misconduct or continual disobedience is a harmful and dangerous example to other students at the school; or
b. because of the student's behavior, it is likely that the student, or other students at the schools, will be seriously harmed if the student is not stood-down or suspended for an unspecified period

While the initial decision is made by a school principal, a school board of trustees is required to undertake independent reviews of decisions to suspend. Where young persons are over sixteen, there may be permanent exclusions from schools.[72] At common law and under the NZBORA such decisions may be judicially reviewable. Even so, the students most commonly excluded are those from Māori and Pacific Island communities as well as from low socioeconomic backgrounds who are less likely to invoke this procedure.

In early cases seeking judicial review, courts showed reluctance to revisit school decisions.[73] Now there is strong evidence of a reverse trend, particularly in relation to the blanket application of school rules.[74]

In *M v. Palmerston North Boys High School*,[75] which concerned the suspension of students for infringing the "no alcohol" rule on a school ski trip, J. McGechan of the High Court sent a clear message in relation to school policies and rules which required mandatory school exclusions. In a note following his judgment, he wrote that in taking such action: "Results must not be fixed instead they must be fair."[76] This standard was adopted by the Ministry of Education in their Guidelines to schools for considering such action under the provisions of the *Education Act 1989* and the accompanying rules.[77]

This principle was affirmed by the High Court in a case which tested not only the standard required for the imposition of disciplinary measures but also the application of the right to freedom of expression under section 14 of the *New Zealand Bill of Rights Act 1990*. In *Battison v. Melloy and The Board of Trustees of St John's College*,[78] J. Collins of the High Court stressed that serious disciplinary consequences must be reserved for "truly serious instances of misconduct."[79]

In that case a failure to comply with a school rule relating to hair length, which importantly was held to lack sufficient precision, fell short of that high threshold aimed at empowering school officials to remove students only when their action seriously impacts on welfare and safety. Actions which serves to disrupt the attendance of children at schools, the court maintained, requires "sound, objective evidence that suspension is necessary,"[80] something absent in this case.

J. Collins allowed judicial review essentially on his belief that the school hair rule was flawed for lack of certainty in its wording and thus was prone to subjective interpretation. In conclusion he posited:

> My conclusion that the School's hair rule breaches the requirements that it be certain provides the school and its wider community with an opportunity to decide whether or not it is necessary for the school to continue to have a hair rule. In considering this issue the School will need to give very careful consideration as to whether or not any hair rule would breach a student's rights to autonomy, individual dignity and his rights to freedom of expression affirmed by s 14 of the *NZBORA*, I have deliberately refrained from commenting on those issues in this judgment.[81]

Strict adherence to due process is required by the courts. In *D v. M and The Board of Trustees of Auckland Grammar School*, J. Smellie determined that the main concern of the court in considering judicial review is the decision-making process and it does not substitute its view on the merits of the case.[82] In *Boviard v. J*, while ruling that it was not necessary in every case for school officials to involve the parents of children in their investigations, the Court of Appeal found this does not diminish insistence on due process.[83] It stressed that it must be satisfied that educators relied on correct facts in making their decisions.

As mentioned above, schools are increasingly faced with complex issues surrounding the discipline of children with disabilities. School officials must balance the right to education of children who demonstrates antisocial behavior arguably as a result of their disabilities, against the right of all students to education in safe environments. Recently, in 2013, the New Zealand Ministry of Education, in its assistance to principals, emphasised the challenges for schools in managing student behaviour when working with students with special education needs, pointing to Individual Education Plans to help support schools to work with students, families and sometimes agencies to support students' access to schooling.[84]

Recognition of the difficulties, and the responsibilities, of schools in this regard was acknowledged by the High Court in *A v. Hutchinson & Board of Trustees of Green Bay High School*.[85] Here J. Faire overturned the action of school authorities who expelled a child with Aspergers syndrome because of his continual anti-social and disruptive behaviour. The final precipitating incident concerned the boy and his skateboard and the disciplinary action taken by members of staff who were aware that in such situations the boy needed time out to destress. The judge found that staff at the school had a responsibility, and the ability, to react differently, to the boy's behavior.

The Court of Appeal dismissed an appeal by the school.[86] This was an example of strategic litigation undertaken with the assistance of Youth Law Aotearoa Inc. While it was essentially a challenge to the process used by the school in its interactions with the boy, it was aimed at enabling a consideration of wider issues surrounding the right to special needs education.[87]

Recently, the High Court has been also asked to intervene where the disciplinary decision of school authorities did not involve exclusion. In the "*St Bedes college case,*"[88] which attracted some media attention, [89] two boys who were in the school's rowing team and on their way to a national regatta committed a criminal offence by jumping on the luggage conveyer belt at the airport. School authorities reacted by removing the boys from the team and requiring them to return to the school.

J. Dunningham granted an interim injunction for the boys on the basis that there were questions relating to whether school authorities complied with the rules of natural justice and whether they had given due consideration to the proportionality of the consequences for the students concerned in the form of alleged being removed from the possibility of being chosen for the national rowing team. This case, it could be said, reflected largely on the socioeconomic standing of the parents prepared to ask a court to overturn the injunction and on the popularity of the sport of rowing. Within the context of school discipline it must be noted that now the seclusion of a child or young person is no longer an acceptable tool for behavior management and is banned under the *Education Act 1989* (section 139AB). Similarly physical restraint is now statutorily recognized as a serious intervention which may only be used in cirumstances which render it absolutely necessary (section 139AC).

The above provisions of the *Education Act 1989*, primarily sections 13 to 19, and the Regulations made under that Act, apply only to state schools, not private schools. In private schools the relationship is contractual with the parents. Still, while challenges to school disciplinary exclusion measures would most likely be framed in breach of contract terms, it is not beyond the realms of possibility that a court would consider a decision to be reviewable where there was evidence of a breach of natural justice in the process.[90]

TEACHERS' EMPLOYMENT AND RIGHTS

Staff members in New Zealand schools have the same rights, as well as responsibilities and duties of all within the education system, pursuant to the *NZBORA* and the *HRA*. While these rights are fundamental, they must be read in conjunction with the statutory responsibilities of principals and

Boards of Trustees for safe educational environments, and rights such as freedom of expression could be held to be subject to this overarching concern. Very often schools tread a fine line. While academic freedom is guaranteed within tertiary education,[91] this does not extend to schools.

This section is confined to the rights associated with teacher employment and the responsibilities associated particularly with the unique position of teachers and all staff.[92] Against this background, three statutes cover teacher employment in state schools in New Zealand. First, the *Education Act 1989* provides that school Boards of Trustees are the employers of all staff and the duties thereunder may be delegated.[93] Importantly, Schedule 6 *Education Act 1989* imposes a wide responsibility to exercise powers in such a way to ensure that all students are able to attain their highest possible standards of educational achievement.

Section 76 provides that principals are the chief executives of their board who must comply with policy directives but otherwise have complete discretion to manage and administer schools on day-to-day bases.[94] The process for teacher registration and deregistration, and disciplinary action in relation to teacher misconduct and teacher competency is also provided for in this Act and are discussed below.[95]

Second, the *State Sector Act 1988* imposes on a board a duty to be a "good employer."[96] Third, The *Employment Relations Act 2000* provides the framework for employment of staff in state and state-integrated schools. It directs that for matters such as a duty of good faith and maintaining a constructive relationship. Importantly the Act requires, in section 103A, compliance with a test of "justification" when considering discipline or dismissal. The Act further mandates an objective determination based on principles of natural justice in relation, for example, to the investigation of grounds and the opportunity given to the teacher to respond.

In considering matters of dismissal, the courts have been concerned to place a "high standard" on Board employers in light of the consequences of dismissal for the teacher not only in terms of their employment but also under the system of registration. The latter is because in dismissing teachers, school Boards of Trustees are bound to notify the Education Council, previously the Teachers Council, in a process discussed below. At the same time, teachers are obligated to notify prospective new employers of their dismissals. This high standard to be adhered to in undertaking the disciplinary process has been emphasised strongly by the Employment Court in *Lewis v. Howick College Board of Trustees*[97] and more recently in *Edwards v. Board of Trustees of Bay of Islands College.*[98]

In addition to disputes relating to unjustified dismissal, the *Employment Relations Act 2000*, and its regulations, set out a process for resolving other disputes such as personal grievances, discrimination, bullying and harassment, and duress. A mediation service is provided by the Ministry of Business, Innovation, and Employment.

While Boards of Trustees are employer of teachers at state schools, conditions of employment are generally covered by Collective Agreements negotiated on their behalf by their unions.[99] Staff in private schools may elect to be part of collective agreements or may enter into individual employment contracts with the Board of Trustees of their schools.[100]

In recent years, as comparative jurisdictions have seen a rising concern surrounding teacher competence and teacher misconduct towards pupils, New Zealand is no different. In response, the Education Council of Aotearoa New Zealand was constituted as an independent statutory body to replace the previous Teachers' Council as the professional organisation for all teachers in the early childhood and compulsory sector. Its stated aim is to provide leadership and to lift the standards in the teaching profession. Importantly, this Council has a function relating to teacher discipline and teacher competence.[101]

Considering complaints and conducting investigations into matters of teacher conduct and teacher competence are two separate and discreet areas. Matters of conduct are considered by a body known as the Complaints Assessments Committee, whereas matters relating to teacher competence are dealt with by a new Competence Authority set up under section 410AA *Education Act 1989* and acting pursuant to rules promulgated by the Education Council under section 388 *Education Act 1989*.

As noted above, the *Education Act 1989* provides that employers, namely Board of Trustees, or in the case of partnership schools, their managing bodies, are mandated to provide reports to the Education Council in a range of circumstances relating to teacher dismissal, teacher conduct, or competence.

In all of the actions it takes in relation to complaints and investigations relating to teachers, the Council is bound by the rules of natural justice and the *Privacy Act 1993*. The rules under which the Education Council operates are currently the *Education Council Rules 2016* which will be updated pursuant to the new provisions in the *Education Act 1989* relating to the new Competence Authority which replaces the previous Competence Assessor provisions.

CURRENT AND EMERGING ISSUES FACING SCHOOLS

Search and Seizure Generally and In Relation to Digital Technology

Searches of students and seizures of their property is a fraught issue in common with comparative jurisdictions. While the *NZBRA* provides strict protection for both staff and students from "unreasonable" searches and seizures, the wide use of digital technology in schools gives rise to many questions such as what may be considered to be property, what is reasonable, and how this works in terms of privacy protection.

As elsewhere, the use of technology to bully and harass poses ever increasing challenges and complexity. In addition, New Zealand schools are likewise not immune from the threat posed to the safety of the school environment by weapons and drugs. In response a need to clarify issues relating to searches and seizures in light of modern circumstances, new Rules and Guidelines were issued in 2013 for the assistance of teachers in dealing with, and hopefully pre-empting, difficult situations.

The starting point in considering schools' powers is the fundamental right of all persons to be secure from unreasonable search and seizure contained in section 21 of the *NZBORA*. It follows then that school authorities must be able to justify any actions as reasonable and necessary to fulfil their responsibilities to maintain safe environments.

An amendment to the *Education Act 1989*[102] allows school authorities to require students to produce, reveal, and surrender items in their possession which are either likely to endanger the safety of others, detrimentally affect learning environments, or be harmful insofar as they pose immediate threats to the physical or emotional safety of anyone. While staff members must have reasonable grounds for the above, it is only a belief that harm may ensue which allows them to conduct searches. Blanket searches are not allowed in any circumstances.

The Act differentiates between an "item" and a "device." A device is something electronic such as a mobile phone, computer, or tablet. Staff may retain devices if surrendered but may not destroy them. An item is anything else including weapons, drugs, and the like; these may be disposed of by staff. Refusals by students to show or surrender items may be followed by disciplinary actions or, if there is belief that they are harmful, searches can be conducted.

Under the Act, searches may only be of outer clothing, not something students are still wearing, and not body searches or "pat-downs." If school authorities believe that serious criminal offences have been committed or are imminent, and drugs or weapons are involved, there is a requirement that the Police are notified and they are able to execute their usual powers in such circumstances.

There has been controversy from time to time when New Zealand school officials have asked contractors to bring trained search dogs into schools. The new Guidelines clarify that such measures may only be used to search schools and not students' property or persons. While the use of force is generally not permitted, the provisions in sections 41 and 48 of the *Crimes Act 1961* continue to apply when teachers are faced with emergency situations and needs to prevent suicides or to defend themselves or others in where serious injury is like to occur. In such a case, the use of whatever force is reasonably necessary in the situation is justified.

In taking all actions, it is important for school authorities to adhere to their responsibilities under the *Privacy Act 1993*. This Act provides principles in relation to the schools dealing with personal information leading to or generated by a search. Principals must ensure confidentiality of all personal information except where disclosure is necessary in the interests of safety and they must respect students' rights to access to that information.

Cyberbullying and Other Misuse of Technology

Schools now are part of the complex, rapidly evolving and deregulated "cyberspace" environment. New challenges arise on daily bases relating to students' use and misuse of the internet for the purposes of bullying, harassment, and other forms of menace and intimidation.

The new legislative provisions and the Guidelines accompanying them relating to searches and seizures described above provide school authorities with some assistance in relating to nefarious use of electronic devices. However, the scope of schools' jurisdiction and responsibility in this regard can very often be problematic.

School officials are striving, within their responsibility for safety, to ensure the safe and responsible use of digital technology, at the same time, encouraging students to use the internet to research, work, and, importantly, to communicate. While the use of the internet through social media is seen to be an effective medium for learning, increasing numbers of schools are faced with incidences of harmful digital behaviour between students. While there are incidences of sexting and other inappropriate uses by way of images, audio and video recording, the most common challenge is that posed by cyberbullying, an infraction which may involve any of these "items."

Cyberbully has been defined as intentional and repeated hostile behavior using digital technology. The primary issue fronting school authorities when dealing with incidents of this kind is whether they have jurisdiction, namely, whether they have the power and responsibility to take action. Other questions may relate to identifying who is actually involved and whether it amounts to criminal conduct. While these questions rarely lend themselves to simple answers, the fundamental inquiry for school officials must be whether a digital activity or content could reasonably be expected to have a negative impact on the safety of the school's "education and emotional environment"[103] and thus on its educational function.

New Zealand courts have not, as yet, had to consider the legality of a school's actions in this regard. At present, schools are able to rely in their actions on the Guidelines for the Surrender and Retention of Property and

Searches 2014, formulated pursuant to section 139AAI of the *Education Act 1989.*[104]

CONCLUSION

This chapter has provided an outline of the law and education in New Zealand. The New Zealand *Education Act 1989* has undergone comprehensive amendment pursuant to the *Education (Update) Amendment Act 2017* and the changes have been incorporated here where possible and relevant. As they become embedded, they will inevitably give rise to many questions. Within its confines, the chapter and the explanation of the changes are necessarily brief, and, for that reason, references are contained in the footnotes which may lead readers to further explanation.

To end here, though, would be telling only part of the story. In New Zealand and internationally, the key to the exercise of the right to education into the future must be through education systems prioritizing and taking the lead in human rights and citizenship education. Most children and young people spend their formative years in school. Arguably that school provides the template for the rest of students' lives, including their ability to function as citizens within a democratic society with a strong sense of human rights and social justice.

The values incorporated within educational systems and simply, the way in which school officials behave, play a significant part in this. Educating for human rights is an integral part of the responsibility of developing citizens for a free, liberal, and democratic societies. This requires both formal classroom teaching and learning along with processes and procedures for practicing citizenship and human rights within school communities.

The New Zealand government has stated that human rights are a central theme of the New Zealand curriculum.[105] In its value statements it sets out to "reflect cultural diversity," and to "recognise the principles of the Treaty of Waitangi" as central. In recognizing that there is much to be done in effectively integrating human rights education and practice in schools,[106] there are increasing nongovernment initiatives underway such as "Building Human Rights Communities in Education *He Whakatu Tika Tangata-a-iwi Whanui,*" established by Amnesty International, the Development Resource Centre, the Human Rights Commission, the Office of Children's Commissioner, and the Peace Foundation.[107]

It is axiomatic that disputes will happen between school authorities and students, some of which have been discussed above, and it is doubtful whether litigation serves any side's best interests. Alternate dispute resolution has a strong role in New Zealand. Currently, aggrieved students in New Zealand and their parents have Youth Law and the Office of the Commissioner for

Children as avenues for advice and counsel, those in state schools also may complain to the Public Service Ombudsperson.

Various agencies such as the Human Rights Commission and the Privacy Commissioner have been referred to above. Yet, there is, from time to time, a call for a specially constituted Education Review Tribunal.[108] The case was made strongly by Commissioner for Children in 2001 stressing the need for an independent body with the ability to review decisions particularly about school exclusion. The Commissioner noted that adults have rights to appeal or review the decisions of authorities in many sectors and it is clearly discriminatory for children and young people to not be able to access this right.

The focus on the need to review decisions of school authorities, especially as to exclusions, has been renewed recently by the organisation Youth Law in its call for an Independent Appeal Tribunal, in line with that in the UK, as a starting point for a wider-ranging Education Review Tribunal.[109] Few would doubt that, in the devolved system of education provision in New Zealand, such an independent body could play a vital role in enhancing the exercise by children and young people of the rights to, and rights in education.

NOTES

1. Professor Sally Varnham, Faculty of Law, University of Technology Sydney, Australia.
2. See Rishworth, P. T. (1996), "Recent Developments in Education Law in New Zealand" Vol 1 (1) *Australia and New Zealand Journal of Law and Education*, 33; New Zealand Law Society CLE publications: Walsh, P., and Greig, A., and Hannah, J. (2016), and Hannah, J., Rishworth, P., and Walsh, P. (2004).
3. This trend may be said to follow other jurisdictions such as the US, UK, and countries of Europe and is reflected in the increase in research in this area shown in the wide range of papers presented at the regular conferences and seminars of the Australia and New Zealand Education Law Association in New Zealand and Australia and in the range of articles printed in the journal of that organisation, the *International Journal of Law and Education* (now in its 20th edition), and also the wide attendance at Law and Education seminars conducted by organizations such as LawSense and as part of the New Zealand Law Society Continuing Legal Education programme.
4. *The Politics of Learning and teaching in Aotearoa New Zealand* (Coxon, E., Jenkins, K., Marshall, J., and Massey, L., eds.) (Dunmore Press, 1994), 44.
5. Article 1 Treaty of Waitangi Te Tiriti o Waitangi.
6. Articles 2 and 3, Treaty of Waitangi Te Tiriti o Waitangi.
7. This is due largely to differences between the Māori wording and the English translation. http://www.NZhistory.net.nz/politics/treaty/the-treaty-in-brief (Ministry for Culture and Heritage, updated 21 January 2016).
8. Report of the Waitangi Tribunal on the te reo Māori Claim (Wai 11) 2nd ed Wellington, New Zealand https://forms.justice.govt.nz/search/Documents/WT/wt_DOC_68482156/Report%20on%20the%20Te%20Reo%20Māori%20Claim%20W.pdf.
9. *The Māori Language Act 1987* came into force on 1 August 1987.
10. This practice was begun around 1847 with the Education Ordinance and in 1867 the *Native Schools Act* was passed by the colonial government to formalise this government funding. For a full discussion of the social and political background to this funding, see Simon J, Historical Perspectives on Schooling. In *The Politics of Learning and teaching in Aotearoa*

New Zealand (Coxon, E., Jenkins, K., Marshall, J. and Massey, L., eds.) (Dunmore Press, 1994), 37–81 at 59–64. It is notable that, although New Zealand education is "secular" religion played a large part in early schooling and in Māori culture. The latter influence remains to this day.

11. The *Secondary Schools Act 1903.*

12. As required by the *Māori Language Act 1975* and the Principles of the Treaty of Waitangi—nga matapono o re tiriti http://www.justice.govt.nz/tribunals/waitangi-tribunal/treaty-of-waitangi/tribunals/waitangi-tribunal/documents/public/treaty-principles-appendix-99.

13. Sections 61–63B *Education Act 1989.* For a full discussion see Rishworth, P. T. (1996) "Recent Developments in Education Law in New Zealand" Vol. 1(1) *Australia and New Zealand Journal of Law and Education* 33.

14. The *Education (Update) Amendment Act 2017* came into effect on May 17, 2017—now incorporated into the *Education Act 1989.* Its changes will take effect gradually from that date to 2020 (changes in effect incorporated here).

15. Section 71, Part 9, and Schedule 6 *Education Act 1989.*

16. Part 12A; sections 156 and 156AA; Part 33 (which repealed the *Private Schools Conditional Integration Act 1975*); sections 35A to 35S, respectively.

17. Note 14. The key provisions for setting up and management of such schools are now set out in part 12A *Education Act 1989.* For a full discussion of charter/partnership schools, see Geohagen, E. (2013), "The New Zealand Model of Charter Schools: A Look at the Legislative Framework and Legal Characteristics of a Partnership School Kura Hourua." Proceedings of the Annual Conference of the Australia and New Zealand Education Law Association, "Safe, Successful and Sustainable Education: Is the Law a Sword or a Shield?" Hobart, Tasmania, Australia, 1–3 October.

18. http://www.education.govt.nz/ministry-of-education/specific-initiatives/partnership-schools-kura-hourua/.

19. Unfortunately outside the limits of this chapter, but see, for example, http://www.nbr.co.nz/article/partnership-schools-dont-be-hasty-ja-135288.

20. The former introduced as section 1A *Education Act 1989*; see https://www.education.govt.nz/ministry-of-education/legislation/the-national-education-guidelines/.

21. Section 60A *Education Act 1989*, National Administration Guideline (NAG) 5a.

22. Rishworth, P. T. "Recent Developments in Education Law in New Zealand (1996) Vol 1 (1) *Australia and New Zealand Journal of Law and Education*, 33–54, 1. However, the newly introduced National Education and Learning Priorities (note 20) to be issued every five years aim for each young person to attain educational achievement to the best of his or her potential and instilling inclusion and diversity (sections 1A (3)(a) and (3)(c)).

23. Part 7A *Education Act 1989*—an extended range of powers and provisions is contained in sections 78H–78S *Education Act 1989.*

24. Sections 78I–78T *Education Act 1989.* For a comprehensive explanation of this area, see Matthews, M. (2015) "Statutory Interventions for State and Integrated Schools," New Zealand Law Society Continuing Legal Education, Education Law Intensive, 61. For an explanation of changes in interventions see https://www.education.govt.nz/ministry-of-education/legislation/the-education-update-amendment-act/.

25. The United Nations Special Rapporteur on the Right to Education from 1998 to 2004, in (2001) Right to Education Primers No 3, "*Human Rights Obligations: making education available, accessible, acceptable and adaptable,*" referred to in *The State of the Right to Education Worldwide-Free or Fee*, 2006 Global Report, 224 and quoted widely.

26. The words of Barangwanath, J. in *Daniels v. Attorney-General*, Unreported Judgment of the High Court of New Zealand, Auckland Registry M1516/SW99, 3 April 2002 (this case concerned a challenge to government policy for the education of children with special needs and is discussed in that context later in this chapter).

27. The Right Hon. Peter Frazer, Prime Minister and leader of the Labour Government of New Zealand 1940–1949.

28. With the *Education Act 1877* and the *Secondary Education Act 1903.*

29. See for example, Simon, J., Historical Perspectives on Schooling. In *The Politics of Learning and teaching in Aotearoa New Zealand* (Coxon, E., Jenkins, K., Marshall, J., and Massey, L., eds.) (Dunmore Press, 1994), 37–81.

30. Sections 11A-11Q *Education Act 1989*. The secretary of education may, where necessary, implement an enrollment scheme sections 11IA *Education Act 1989*.

31. Section 8 *Education Act 1989*

32. "Special Education Policy Principles," Ministry of Education Te Tahuhu o Te Matauranga, 2015, https://www.education.govt.nz/ministry-of-education/overall-strategies-and-policies/special-education-policy-principles/.

33. *Daniels v. Attorney-General* (3 April 2002), Unreported Judgment of the High Court of New Zealand, Auckland Registry M1516/SW99, per Baragwanath, J.

34. *Attorney-General v. Daniels* [2003] 2 NZLR 741 (CA). For a comprehensive discussion of this decision, see Ryan, E. J. (2004), "Failing the system? Enforcing the right to education in New Zealand," *Victoria University of Wellington Law Review (VUWLR)*, 45, 735; and Varnham, S. (2005), "*Daniels v. The Attorney-General: Children with Special Needs and the Right To Education in New Zealand,* " 1(2) *International Journal of Education Law and Policy*, 236.

35. *"A" v. Hutchinson & The Board of Trustees of Green Bay High School* [2014] NZHC 253 (19 February 2014).

36. New Zealand Parliament Aotearoa, "Inquiry into the identification and support for students with significant challenges of dyslexia, dyspraxia, and autism spectrum disorders in primary and secondary schools," Report of the Education and Science Committee to the House of Representatives, November 2016. https://www.parliament.nz/resource/en-NZ/51DBSCH_SCR71769_1/cd88907f3c87d07b8b1db046417ed1e43fcd3e85.

37. Education Review Office, "Inclusive practices for students with special education needs in schools (March 2015) 05/03/2015." http://www.ero.govt.nz/National-Reports/Inclusive-practices-for-students-with-special-education-needs-in-schools-March-2015/National-report-summary.

38. Section 60A *Education Act 1989*, NAG 5a.

39. Although, Board members are not individually criminally liable as are "officers" (such as the school principal) they must be proactive in understanding the risks of all entering the school, including those posed by chemicals and stress. For more information see Mitchell, S. (2015), *Current Issues in Education and the Law: Proposed Changes to Health and Safety Law*. Seminar conducted by the Australia and New Zealand Education Law Association (ANZELA) 25 June. See also http://www.education.gpvt.nz/ministry-of-education/specific-initiatives/health-and-safety-legislation.

40. "Personal Injury" as covered by the Act now has extremely broad definition set out primarily in sections 25 and 26.

41. For further information see http://www.acc.co.nz.

42. *The Injury Prevention, Rehabilitation, and Compensation Amendment Act (No.2) 2005*

43. *The Injury Prevention, Rehabilitation, and Compensation Amendment Act 2008*. Both now within the principal Act, sections 21–21B *Accident Compensation Act 2001*.

44. Home education is beyond the confines of this article but for a comprehensive discussion of home education in Australia and New Zealand see Varnham, S. (2008), "My home, my school, my island: Home education in Australia and New Zealand," 23 *PUBLIC SPACE: The Journal of Law and Social Justice* 1, quoting Harding, T. and Farrell, A. (2003), "Home Schooling and Legislated Education," *Australia and New Zealand Journal of Law and Education* 128.

45. http://www.education.govt.nz/bullyingprevention.

46. Australia's Constitution contains an anti-establishment clause, Clause 116, which provides: "The Commonwealth shall not make any law for establishing any religion, or for imposing any religious observance, or for prohibiting the free exercise of any religion, and no religious test shall be required as a qualification for any office or public trust under the Commonwealth." In *Attorney-General (Vic): Ex Rel Black v. The Commonwealth (the DOGs case)* the funding of denominational, Catholic schools was challenged unsuccessfully on the basis that it amounted to the "establishment" of religion by the State prohibited by Clause 116. More recently in connection with freedom from religion the High Court was asked to consider

whether the Commonwealth Government's funding of the School Chaplaincy Program, introduced in 2007 in all public schools, was in breach of Clause 116: *Williams v. Commonwealth of Australia* [2012] HCA 23 (20 June 2012) and [2014] HCA 23. The High Court avoided this issue by basing its decision on other grounds and subsequently such funding has been enabled by legislative provision.

47. Section 77 *Education Act 1964* and following provisions making provision for religious instruction.

48. Part 33, section 414(1) *Education Act 1989*.

49. Clarification of the charges which may be levied on students by these schools was achieved in 2012 by a Declaratory Judgment of the High Court of New Zealand in *New Zealand Catholic Education Office Limited v. Attorney-General* [2012] NZHC 793 (27 April 2012). An interesting account of the history of Catholic School integration may be found in an Affidavit presented to the High Court on behalf of the Catholic Education Office by Patrick Lynch the Chief Executive Officer http://www.nzceo.catholic.org.nz/media/resources/brief-history-of-integration.pdf.

50. It should be noted that the *Education Act 1989* (with 2017 amendments) is the most recent legislation but it preserves some provision from the *Education Act 1964*. For a comprehensive discussion of the place of religion in schools in the increasingly diverse nature of New Zealand society, both religiously and culturally, particularly with an appreciable growth in recent years of Hindu, Buddhist, and Muslim communities, see a publication by the New Zealand Human Rights Commission and Victoria University of Wellington, note 51 below.

51. See Human Rights Commission (2009), *"Religion in New Zealand Schools: Questions and concerns" Te Kahui Tika Tangata* and Victoria University of Wellington, New Zealand.

52. Sections 77–80, *Education Act 1964*.

53. In the 2013 Census 48.5 percent (10,869 people) stated they had no religion, while 5.7 percent (1,287 people) objected to answering the religion question—Statistics New Zealand. http://www.stats.govt.nz/searchresults.aspx?q=religious%20profiles.

54. Varnham, S. and Evers, M. (2009), "Secular, Singular and Self-Expression? Religious Freedom in Australian and New Zealand Education," 28(3) *Irish Educational Studies* 292, quoting Rishworth, P. T. (2007), *The Religious Clauses of the New Zealand Bill of Rights*. Essay presented at the Legal Research Foundation's Conference "The New Zealand Bill of Rights Comes of Age," 27–28 July, in Auckland, New Zealand, 3.

55. Note 51.

56. Note 51.

57. A Māori incantation or prayer which acknowledges a spiritual presence.

58. There has been discussion whether Māori Christianity and spirituality generally, in the form of prayers at Māori ceremonies, should be allowed in schools, see Human Rights Commission Report (2004), *Human Rights in New Zealand Today Nga Tika Tangata O Te Motu*.

59. Many of its reviews and reports are cited within different contexts within this chapter.

60. It must be noted however that while this Act, in common with the UK's *Human Rights Act 1990*, is not supreme law, it has been accorded significant status by the New Zealand courts—see for example, the words of Cooke, J. in *Simpson v. Attorney-General (Baigent's case)* [1994] 3 NZLR 667 when monetary compensation was awarded for unreasonable search and seizure in breach of section 21 *NZBORA*.

61. Section 3(b) *New Zealand Bill of Rights Act 1990* as they are performing a "public function, power or duty conferred" by law. Certainly there has been strong support of its impact at least in public schools as authorities performing a public function pursuant to s 3(b) NZBORA: *RE Strip Search at Hastings Boys High School* 1 NZBORR 480 (Commissioner for Children). Despite McGechan, J. holding in the case of *Federated Farmers of NZ v. New Zealand Post Ltd* 3 NZBORR 339 that s3(b) ensured applicability to private bodies engaged in a public function, there was doubt cast by Goddard J in relation to full applicability to public schools" actions in a boarding facility attached to the school—Goddard J in *McGuinn v. Board of Trustees of Palmerston North Boys' High School and Attorney-General* (H. C., Palmerston North, 24-12-96; CP 36/95). However, at least in the context of search and seizure at school and the section 21 *NZBORA*, the Guidelines for the Surrender and Retention of Public Property and Search, January 2014, make it clear that the 2013 provisions of the *Education Act 1989*-

sections 139AAA–139AAI in the case of public schools and in hostels run by those schools, are subject to the Act.

62. Pursuant to section 145 *HRA*.

63. For example, *"A" v. Hutchinson* [2014] NZHC 253 (19 February 2014). This is unlike, for example, the case of *Purvis v. NSW* in Australia in which the issues relating to suspension and expulsion of a child with special needs were argued as alleged breaches of the relevant provisions of the *Disability Discrimination Act 1992* (Cth).

64. New Zealand Human Rights Commission *te Kahui Tika Tangata* (2009), *"Disabled Children's Right To Education,"* Wellington, New Zealand.

65. New Zealand Human Rights Commission *te Kahui Tika Tangata* (2009), *"Disabled Children's Right To Education,"* Wellington, New Zealand, 19.

66. The Māori word for family.

67. Note 34.

68. See the submission of the Human Rights Commission, and the Report Recommendations summary, pp. 7–11, note 34. See the New Zealand Government's Response, February 2017 https://www.parliament.nz/en/pb/papers-presented/current-papers/document/PAP_72401/government-response-to-report-of-the-education-and-science where it substantially accepted the recommendations, yet to be implemented.

69. For statistics see http://www.educationcounts.govt.nz. See also http://www.stats.govt.nz/browse_for_stats/people_and_communities/pacific_peoples/pacific-progress-education/schooling.aspx.

70. Section 18AA. Note *Education Act 1989* Sections 139A and 139AB prohibit corporal punishment and seclusion, and Section 137AC limits the use of physical restraint. For material containing practical advice for parents and caregivers on school discipline see Darlow, N., *Schools and the Right to Discipline: A Guide for Parents and Caregivers* (5th ed.) Wellington Community Law Centre, 2011.

71. (2009) *Guidelines for principals and boards of trustees on stand-downs, suspensions, exclusions and expulsions, Part 1 Legal Obligations and Duties. Appendix 1*, 32.

72. Section 17. Sections 17A–18 contain provisions relating to notice, re-enrollment, etc., of stood-down, suspended, expelled, and excluded students.

73. See particularly *Maddever v. Umawera School Board of Trustees* [1993] 2 NZLR 478, and *D v. M and Board of Trustees of Auckland Grammar School* [2003] NZAR 726. For discussion, see Caldwell, J. (2006), "Judicial Review of School Discipline" 22 *New Zealand University Law Review* 240. Rishworth, P. and Breakwell, J. (2016), "Judicial Review of Internal Decisions in State Schools," Proceedings of the Annual Conference of the Australia and New Zealand Education Law Association, Auckland, New Zealand, September.

74. For a discussion of school exclusionary measures for discipline, see Varnham, S. (2004–2005), "Getting Rid of Troublemakers" Vol 9(2) *Australian and New Zealand Journal of Law and Education* 53.

75. [2003] NZAR 705 (1990).

76. Ibid. p. 725.

77. Education (Stand-Down, Suspension, Exclusion, and Expulsion) Rules 1999. For a case evidencing that standard, see *Boviard & the Board of Trustees of Lynfield College v. J (Suing by his Litigation Guardian)* [2008] NZCA 325 (19 May 2008) per O'Regan, Priestley, and Heath, J. J.

78. [2014] NZHC 1462 (27 June 2014). It is important to note that as an "integrated" school under the *Private Schools Conditional Integration Act 1975* St. John's School is bound by all the provisions of the *Education Act 1989* and other education legislation, as a state school.

79. Ibid. para. 85.

80. Ibid. para. 563.

81. Ibid. para. 96.

82. [2003] NZAR 726 (HC), at p. 731.

83. [2008] NZAR 667.

84. New Zealand Ministry of Education *Te Tahuku o te Mataurenga* http://www.minedu.govt.nz/NZEducation/EducationPolicies/Schools/StanddownsSuspensionsExclusionsExpulsions/PartTwo/

Section2CreatingProceduresAndProcesses.aspx. See the earlier discussion relating to education and special needs, note 68.

85. *"A" v. Hutchinson & The Board of Trustees of Green Bay High School* [2014] NZHC 253 (19 February 2014).

86. *Hutchinson v. A* [2015] NZCA 214 (5 June 2015).

87. A recent and comprehensive discussion of this case and others in the context of the issues surrounding special needs education in New Zealand is contained in Puah, J., (2014-2015), "Barriers to Inclusive Education n New Zealand: Enforcing a Right to Special Education" Vol 19(2) & Vol 20(1), 53.

88. [2015] NZHC 536.

89. Nicole Mathewson, Myles Hume, and Brittany Mann, St. Bede's College parents win interim court injunction, *The Press*, March 23, 2015, available at http://www.stuff.co.nz/the-press/news/67473960/st-bedes-college-parents-win-interim-court-injunction.

90. Contrast the Australian situation in *Bird v. Campbelltown Anglican Schools Council* [2007] NSWSC 1419 where the New South Wales Supreme Court held that the decision of a private school was not judicially reviewable.

91. Sections 160 and 161 *Education Act 1989.*

92. For example, there may be circumstances where exercise of the right to freedom of expression or association by a teacher may be held to threaten that safety and could amount to misconduct, although the test for disciplinary action would be strict in light of the threat to a teacher's livelihood: *Lewis v. Howick College Board of Trustees* (2010) NZMC 4.

93. Part 9 and Schedule 6 *Education Act 1989.*

94. In *Hobday v. Timaru Girls High Board of Trustees* (1994) 1 ERNZ 724 the demarcation between the roles of boards and principals was considered and reinforced by the Employment Court, shortly after the inception of the new system of devolution set out in the Government's "Tomorrow's schools" policy and legislated in the *Education Act 1989.*

95. As substantially amended by the *Education (Update) Amendment Act 2017* and now incorporated within the *Education Act 1989* sections 376–413.

96. Section 77A *State Sector Act 1988.*

97. (2010) NZMC 4.

98. (2015) NZMC 3 (3 February 2015). For a comprehensive discussion of employment law relating to teachers, see Harrison, R. (2015), "Employment Law Update" *Education Law Intensive* New Zealand Law Society Continuing Legal Education 33.

99. For example, for primary teachers and principals (years 1 to 7) it is the New Zealand Educational Institute, whereas for secondary teachers and principals (years 8 to 13) it is the Post Primary Teachers' Association and the Secondary Principals' Association of New Zealand. There are other collective agreements for staff in a variety of other school settings, such as special residential schools, therapists, and special assistance teachers and are school staff.

100. The provisions relating to employment of staff in the range of other schools such as private and partnership schools which make up the compulsory education sector are outside the parameters of this chapter. The discussion here is necessary a very limited overview with a focus on the rights and responsibilities of teachers employed within the New Zealand compulsory education sector.

101. Part 32 *Education Act 1989.* It must be noted, however, that the previous Teachers Council was constituted with a similar function and it could be said to be a political show of "muscle" by the current government and Minister of Education.

102. Now incorporated as section 139AAI *Education Act 1989.*

103. In the wording of National Administration Guideline (NAG) 5.

104. In terms of assisting in the management of digital technology there is also a guide http://www.education.govt.nz/school/managing-and-supporting-students/student-behaviour.

105. Human Rights and the New Zealand Curriculum (2007), *Rights, Respect and Responsibilities*, www.rightsined.org.nz.

106. The New Zealand Human Rights Commission (2010), Human Rights in New Zealand 2010—Nga Tika Tangata O Aotearoa, Wellington, New Zealand.

107. Although this is a voluntary program, the small number of schools who participated recorded considerable success in terms of improvement in classroom behavior, reduction in bullying and higher personal expectations of behavior.
108. Media Release Office of the Commissioner for Children Annual Report, Commissioner for Children 7 November 2001.
109. (2012) "Out of School, Out of Mind: The need for an Independent Education Review Tribunal" Youth Law Tino Rangatiratanga Taitamariki.

Chapter Four

Singapore

Mui Kim Teh and Sook May Chia

INTRODUCTION

Singapore, located at the southern tip of Malaysia, is often referred to as the "Red Dot" because of its size. Singapore was founded in 1819 by Sir Stamford Raffles and was, for more than 140 years, a British colony. Singapore joined the Malaysian Federation in 1963, but the merger was short-lived. Singapore became fully independent in 1965 (Gopinathan, 1995). An island of 719 square kilometers, Singapore has a population of approximately 5.4 million with an indigenous population comprising mainly Chinese, Malays, and Indians (Contact Singapore, 2015). Since gaining independence, Singapore has become one of the most prosperous countries in Southeast Asia with a per capita GDP of US $307.9 billion (World Bank, 2015).

Apart from some fish and deep water ports, Singapore has no exploitable natural resources (CIA World Fact Book, 2014/2015). Consequently, in order to achieve economic growth, Singapore has to rely on foreign capital, technology, and "brainpower" to drive its economic system and to access the most lucrative global markets (Tan & Teh, 2013). The government also embraced the ideologies of multiculturalism and meritocracy as sacred principles (Chong, 2010), which arguably play a huge part in Singapore's success.

Singapore's national development policies thus included investments in public education, since, together with innovation, it is seen as a significant economy driver. In fact, the total expenditure for education is about 20 percent of the country's annual budget, second only to its defense spending. Decisions on educational matters, from the primary to university level, are made at a national level by the Ministry of Education (MOE) (Teh & Chia, 2011). Policies are initiated to nurture students in order that the nation has future leaders to meet the challenges of an increasingly service- and knowledge-based economy (Teh & Stott, 2009).

Singapore's education system is regarded as one of the best in the world,[1] attributed largely to the government's stewardship of education policy through the MOE. English was adopted as the primary language of instruction because it was seen as a vital tool in "Singapore's effort to make the world its marketplace" (Lee et al., 2008), as well as a unifying force for the different ethnic groups and cultures (Teh & Stott, 2009), with second language made compulsory in primary schools from 1960 and in secondary schools from 1966 (Lee, 2008).

Education in Singapore is, therefore, strongly policy driven by the government with the MOE controlling the development and administration of publicly funded government or government-aided schools from primary to university levels. It also sets policy for the private education sector.

SOURCES OF EDUCATION LAW

Singapore is a constitutional democracy. Parliament is elected by the people, and the cabinet chosen by the Prime Minister from elected Members of Parliament. The Singaporean Constitution is the fundamental law of the country, where the people's rights are protected.[2] Insofar as education is vital for economic survival after independence, the Constitution recognizes the need to provide education for all, regardless of their ethnic background or socioeconomic status.[3]

The education scene in Singapore in the early twentieth century was characterized by onerous regulatory interventions to control Chinese language schools because the Chinese-educated tended to be more politically active (Gwee & Doraisamy, 1969; Turnbull, 1977). The first legislation to make a significant improvement to the education system was the Education Ordinance 1957, later renamed Education Act. The Schools Regulations and Grant-in-Aid Regulations under this legislation set out the minimum standards for all schools and extended monetary aid to all qualified schools.

The Education (Schools) Regulations (E(S)R) contain strict licensing regulations and conditions for teacher registration so as to achieve their objectives of establishing a common education system for the nation, with English as the main medium of instruction, and promoting nationalistic values and economic growth (Teh & Stott, 2009). Issues such as the appointment of principals and teachers, school premises, playgrounds, classrooms and equipment, school workshops and science laboratories, and health matters, such as lavatories, water supply, and food vendors are regulated. Section 111 of the E(S)R also prohibits political propaganda in schools and control of use of textbooks by any particular group beyond the MOE by requiring syllabi to be approved by the Director-General of Education.

Schools in Singapore are classified as either "government" or "government-aided," with the former being fully funded, while the latter, usually religious schools, receive partial funding. The Education (Grant-In-Aid) Regulations (E(GIA)R), the subsidiary legislation of the Education Act, enables the government to render financial aid to government-aided schools, provided they comply with the standards stipulated in the Regulations. In order to ensure consistency and a good standard of teaching across the nation, section 14 of the E(GIA)R requires these aided schools to obtain the MOE's approval before they employ prospective teachers.

In the late 1980s, the MOE introduced independent schools to provide for greater parental choices. These comprised outstanding government schools or government-aided schools, and they were given autonomy to decide on matters such as curriculum, admission of students, management, and funding (Ng, 2007). Additional government funding is allotted to these schools to expand their resources and curricula.

In 1994, the MOE introduced "autonomous schools." These were schools tending to have outstanding academic results and were given autonomy over specified aspects of curriculum and administration. While no legislative interventions were enacted to implement this program, by having this status, 10 percent more in annual per capita government grants was given to them (Ng, 2007).

The Education Endowment and Savings Schemes Act was first enacted in 1992 to provide government funding for students to use on enrichment activities. All Singaporean students in MOE-funded schools, namely government and government-aided schools, government-funded independent, and special education schools qualified for the funds. In 2014, the eligibility to receive these contributions was extended to all Singaporean children aged seven to sixteen, including those not studying in MOE-funded schools.[4]

The success of an education system depends very much on quality teachers. As such, the law ensures that tight control is exercised over the employment and discipline of teachers. Article 110 of the Singapore Constitution empowers the Public Service Commission (PSC) "to appoint, confirm . . . and exercise disciplinary control over public officers." However, under Article 116 of the Constitution, in particular, the Public Service Commission Delegation of Disciplinary Functions, Directions, the PSC may delegate its disciplinary functions to another public officer; consequently, this function is ordinarily delegated to the Permanent Secretary of the MOE.

Teachers who are public servants appointed by the PSC cannot be dismissed or disciplined without adherence to the Public Service (Disciplinary Proceedings) Regulations. For non-public servants, the terms of their contracts with their schools controls.

An interesting piece of legislation is s 88 of the E(S)R on corporal punishment. While no corporal punishment is permissible on girl pupils, corporal punishment of boy pupils can be administered with a light cane on the palms of the hands or on the buttocks over the clothing. Nevertheless, schools are given strict guidelines by the MOE on how and when to administer such punishment.[5]

INSTITUTIONAL ISSUES

Compulsory Education

In the early years, the Singaporean government recognized the need to provide every child with at least six years of education from the age of six (Goh & Gopinathan, 2008). Yet education was not compulsory in Singapore. Nevertheless, because nearly all Singaporeans sent their children to school,[6] there seemed to be little need for legislation to intervene. However, in 2003, the Compulsory Education Act (CEA) was introduced for primary schools. This was probably either in response to the United Nations Convention on the Rights of the Child (Teh & Stott, 2009), or, in the view of one commentator, a response to parents withdrawing their children from mainstream schools in favor of religious-based education and homeschooling (Chan, 2007).

A child of compulsory school age refers to one above the age of six years who has not yet attained the age of fifteen years. Under the CEA, it is a criminal offense if parents fail to enroll their Singapore-born children in "National primary schools"[7] and to ensure their regular attendance in these schools. Provisions in the Act do allow parents to apply for exemptions with or without conditions.

The minister may grant exemptions for children to be homeschooled if the curriculum is approved by the Director-General of Education, and for children to attend religious schools provided certain minimum educational standards are observed.[8] Children with special needs, meaning those with physical/intellectual disabilities, preventing them from attending national schools are exempted from compulsory education altogether. Sections 5 and 6 of the CEA provides for the establishment of the Compulsory Education Board to investigate contraventions of the act and to make recommendations to the Director-General of Education regarding the enforcement of its provisions.

Funding

Education in Singapore is financed almost entirely from state revenues. The Singaporean government spent nearly a third of the budget on education during its first nine years in power from 1959 to 1968 (Turnbull, 1977). In the first year of independence, 1965, the government spent $113 million on education. The government allocated 59 percent of the annual education budget to primary education, 27 percent to secondary education, and 14 percent to higher education (Goh & Gopinathan, 2008).

Since 1965 and in recent years, overall public spending[9] on education in Singapore continues to increase. For example, public expenditure on education in 1981 was $942 million; this amount was increased to $11 billion in 2013 (Singapore's Open Data Portal, 2015). Public spending in 2013 as a total percentage of GDP in Singapore was measured at 2.19 (UNESCO Institute of Statistics, 2015) and accounted for 11.6 percent of the government's total expenditure (Ministry of Finance 2014, p. 9). The public expenditure on education has also consistently been the second highest, after defense, in the government's annual fiscal budgets. In the 2015 budget, for example, expenditure on education claimed a 12.1 percent share, compared with 13.1 percent for defense (Ministry of Finance, 2015).

Governing Boards

Education in Singapore is managed mainly by the MOE. The MOE directs the formulation and implementation of education policies while controlling the development and administration of government or government-aided primary schools, secondary schools, and junior colleges; it also registers private schools. However, there are high-achieving government schools that are given the title of independent schools. In order to operate independently, these schools need to acquire separate legal entities. The School Boards Incorporation Act 1990 (SBIA) enables such schools to be incorporated and enter into legal transactions. Once this is completed, these schools cease to be government departments and operate independently of the government.

Public and Non-public Schools

Children begin their education in Singapore from the age of four in a preschool. They commence compulsory primary schooling at the ages of seven to twelve. Primary schools in Singapore are either government or government-aided schools. Students with special education needs attend special schools run by voluntary welfare organizations.[10]

Secondary education in Singapore is for students from thirteen to sixteen years of age with a wide range of schools from which to choose. In addition to government and government-aided, independent, and autonomous secondary schools, there are specialized schools, the integrated program, specialized independent schools along with private schools and institutions.

Specialized schools offer customized programs for students who are more suited to practical learning, while specialized independent schools focus on students with aptitudes for mathematics and science, inclinations for applied learning and creativity, exceptional ability in sports or the arts.[11] The integrated program (IP) provides an integrated six-year secondary and junior college (post-secondary) education for students who are academically strong. These students are taught beyond the academic curriculum with the aim of stretching their potential in non-academic areas. The IP leads to the GCE A-level qualification or other diplomas.

The final option is that of private schools and institutions. Although these schools and institutions offer their own curricula, before they can operate, they are required to obtain registration from the MOE in accordance with the regulations in the Private Education Act (Cap 247A).

Safety and Liability

It is established law in Singapore that school authorities are required to exercise a duty of care to safeguard the physical health and safety of their students by protecting them from all reasonably foreseeable risks of injury or harm. Safety issues leading to liability in negligence can easily arise from the lack of or inadequate supervision in a variety of school activities and settings. These activities and settings may include classrooms, physical education lessons, science laboratory activities, craft workshops, cookery classes, art classes, activities before and after school hours, school grounds, sports activities, and field trips.

In Singapore, no specific legislation deals with the health, safety, and welfare of students in schools. However, the common law of negligence and occupier's liability, combined with the numerous guidelines in the Principal's Handbook on safety, provide at least some guidance on the standard of care required by educators.

Singaporeans are not commonly litigious. Until 2007, all civil cases brought against schools had been settled out of court.[12] The first civil case brought by parents against the government for negligence and breach of the duty of care was heard by the Singapore courts in September 2007.[13] Following this case, suits taken against schools for negligence, but they were still generally settled out of court.[14]

In 2015, a former student of a secondary school sued officials for failing to protect her from being bullied, resulting in her continuing her studies at a prestigious school in England. The student sued for pain and suffering as well as for the school fees in England. At the time of writing, the matter has not been resolved. Although reported cases on safety and liability in Singapore are few, the duty of care of schools and the safety of students are gaining increasing prominence.

FACULTY RIGHTS

Due Process

Hiring

Education plays a vital role in Singapore. In order to attract quality teachers, the MOE ensures that remuneration is competitive[15] with avenues for fast promotions (Goh & Lee, 2008). The MOE employs teachers from three groups of applicants in the hiring process: those without teaching qualifications, those with teaching qualifications, and those who are former MOE-trained teachers. Successful applicants in the first category undergo training at the National Institute of Education (NIE), a part of Nanyang Technological University. Those who do not meet the necessary academic requirements for the respective NIE programs need to pass an additional Entrance Proficiency Test. Applicants with a teaching qualification or who are formerly MOE trained do not need to undergo further training.

Singaporean teachers in government schools and some in aided schools are civil servants. This means that on appointment, these teachers are subject to the usual terms and conditions of civil servants and public disciplinary regulations governing their employment.

In 2001, the Education Service Incentive Payment Act was enacted to encourage long service, experience, and commitment in teaching. Under this legislation, a scheme known as the Connect Plan was established allowing teachers working in government and government-aided schools to qualify in Singapore for "awards," annual monetary contributions to teachers below the "superscale" grade in the Education Service.[16] The amount of contribution is determined by the length and continuity of service and other qualifying conditions stipulated in the regulations such as not having any criminal record or not being guilty of professional misconduct.

Promotion and Tenure

The Enhanced Performance Management System (EPMS) was introduced in 2005 to assess the quality of Singapore's teachers. EPMS, a model based on competency, assesses the knowledge, skills, and professional characteristics of teachers in three "fields of excellence" (Goh & Lee, 2008). Teachers are promoted through three tracks: the teaching track, the leadership track, and the senior specialist track.

Teachers are able to move across different career tracks so long as they meet their respective standards and criteria. At the apex of the teaching track is principal master teacher while the highest position in the leadership track is that of Director-General of Education at the MOE. The specialist track is geared toward specialized areas where deep knowledge and skills are essential for breaking new ground in educational developments; this work usually takes place at the MOE. The highest position in this track is chief specialist.

Tenure

The term *tenure* is not used in the Singapore's context. The term is also not found in human resource policy and guidelines governing the recruitment, hiring, and firing of teachers in Singapore. Newly trained teachers from NIE are generally assured of a permanent emplacement after a year's probation in their first schools. During this one year, principals assesses whether the teachers achieved satisfactory levels of performance to be employed as permanent staff, that is, deemed to be emplaced under "Permanent Establishment." Those who do not meet expectations are counseled and given various forms of support to improve, failing which they must leave the teaching service.

Crucially, only NIE-trained teachers emplaced under Permanent Establishment are considered for advancement in the different career tracks and higher appointments. In addition to these opportunities for career advancement, teachers have access to a range of professional development schemes and are eligible for the Connect Plan, which allows them to receive payouts at various defined points in their career. More importantly, teachers under Permanent Establishment cannot be fired without just cause because the grounds for dismissal are clearly spelled out in the human resource policy and guidelines. This issue is now addressed in greater detail.

Dismissal

The dismissal of teachers in Singapore, although rare, does happen occasionally. The most common grounds for dismissal are professional misconduct and poor performance. An example of the former is inappropriate relationships with students. Teachers who engage in such behavior are subject to disciplinary action, which usually leads to dismissal and debarment from future employment with the MOE. Other examples of professional misconduct are meting out corporal punishment without appropriate approval, committing a criminal offense, and neglect of duty. Ultimately, what constitutes "misconduct" is determined by the Inquiry Committee appointed by the Public Service Commission.

With regard to poor performance, the EPMS "ranks" teachers into the performance bands of "A to E," with "D" and "E" deemed as underperforming. To ensure that the system is fair, a ranking panel, comprising the principal, vice principal(s) and heads of departments, with a cluster superintendent, namely a senior officer who supervises a group of schools, as moderator, is convened before the ranking procedure is finalized (Teh & Stott, 2009). A teacher receiving an "E" performance grade is put on a Performance Review

Process (PRP) which lasts for nine months. The PRP comprises two phases: Phase 1, for six months and Phase 2, for three months. The teacher is taken off the PRP if his or her performance improves at the end of either Phase 1 or 2. If teachers do not improve after Phase 2, the MOE takes action to terminate their service.

The rules for teachers in non-government schools in Singapore are different than those for their colleagues in government schools. For these teachers, the terms of their contracts with their school determines the reasons and procedures for dismissal.

Freedom of Speech

Under Article 14(1)(a) of the Singapore Constitution, all citizens of Singapore have the right to freedom of speech and expression. The government still may impose by law such "restrictions as it considers necessary or expedient in the interest of the security of Singapore . . . , public order or morality and restrictions designed to protect . . . against contempt of court, defamation or incitement to any offence" (Article 14(2)(a)).

No laws restrict teachers from exercising this freedom. Yet teachers are expected to conduct themselves in a manner upholding the integrity of the public service. Teachers are therefore expected to act within the policies governing public officers. This may include seeking consent from the MOE before agreeing to make or provide any form of broadcast or television appearances relating directly or indirectly to the teacher's official work. The MOE is understandably keen to monitor comments that may be seen to represent the views of the government.

In June 2003, the government issued a report, "The Remaking of Singapore," which acknowledged that, out of economic necessity, there is an urgency for a change of mindset of Singaporeans. The report states that "the centre of gravity, of power, will alter, the rules of engagement will change and OB (out of bounds) markers, the avenues for expressions, regulations, all these will change" (Lee, 2003). This has been met with skepticism as many observe that members of the People's Action Party government continue to "bring defamation suits to defend their integrity, lest they lose their moral authority" (Thio, 2012). This suggests that free speech is subject to protecting the reputations of politicians. Accordingly, there is still a perception that freedom of speech is restricted in Singapore. This was evidenced in 2013, when the MOE conducted ten dialogue sessions with 716 educators, exchanging views on education and the future of Singapore in 2030.

The general consensus is that there needs to be more freedom of speech and that the government needs to have greater tolerance for different views (Ministry of Education, 2013). However, the MOE argues that the climate for free speech for teachers has improved, insofar as they are not only given the opportunity to be involved in school processes, but are also afforded many platforms to express their views. One such platform is the online forum for teachers where a wide range of views are discussed such as teacher grading, school ranking, and life in schools (Teh & Stott, 2009).

Freedom of Association/ Unions

Article 14(1)(b) of the Singapore Constitution grants all citizens of Singapore the right to assemble peaceably and to form associations. Even so, the government may impose "such restrictions as it considers necessary or expedient in the interest of the security of Singapore or . . . public order or morality," and the "restrictions on the right to form associations . . . may also be imposed by any law relating to labour or education" (Article 14[2][b] and [c]).

Teachers in Singapore are certainly not restricted from forming associations and, in fact, they have different teachers unions from which to choose, the largest of which is the Singapore Teachers' Union (STU).[17] Unlike most jurisdictions, though, the relationship between the teachers' unions and the government is more collaborative and cooperative than adversarial (Teh & Stott, 2009).

Religious Freedom

Article 15(1) of the Singaporean Constitution provides all persons the right to profess and practice their religions and to propagate their beliefs. Yet, as a secular and multiracial country, the MOE strictly prohibits teachers in Singapore from proselytizing to students in schools. Even mission schools must follow MOE's policy of allowing prayers, religious classes, chapel, or Mass to be optional. Also, students cannot be required to be involved in religious activities as a condition for school admission. The religious freedom of teachers to profess and practice their religion is thereby subject to the national interest of maintaining the multicultural and multireligious sensitivity and harmony in Singapore (Teh & Stott, 2009, p. 181).

Anti-discrimination Protection

Anti-discrimination law in Singapore is largely found in Article 12(1) of the Singapore Constitution, according to which all persons are equal before the law and entitled to the equal protection of the law. Further, Article 12(2) prohibits discrimination against citizens of Singapore on the grounds only of religion, race, descent, and/or place of birth in any law or in the appointment to any office or employment under a public authority.

Apart from the constitutional protections, this area of law is determined by common law. In *Public Prosecutor v. Taw Cheng Kong* (1998), the Court of Appeal, the highest court in Singapore, interpreted Article 12(1) to mean that all persons *in like situations* are to be treated alike rather than that all persons are to be treated equally (italics ours). This perhaps explains the position the Singapore government had with regard to the hiring of homosexuals by the public service, including teachers.

Insofar as gay sex is illegal in Singapore,[18] the government refused to employ homosexuals for a long time if prospective employees' sexual orientation were known (Arnold, 2003). This policy reflects the prevailing conservatism of the Confucian ethnic of the Chinese minority as well as the Muslim Malay minority.

As such, homosexual teachers employed by the MOE would need to keep their sexual orientation secret. This changed in 2003 when the then Prime Minister Goh Chok Tong, in an interview with *Time* magazine, announced that gays and lesbians would be allowed to work in the civil service provided they disclosed their sexual preferences (Weiss, 2015). Interestingly, while Singapore has shown greater openness toward the gay community, it has nevertheless left the issue of the tension between declaring one's sexual preference and its criminality unresolved.

STUDENT RIGHTS

Admission Process

Because primary education is compulsory in Singapore, parents of children who are at least six years old on January 1 of the year of admission to primary school must register their children in schools during the Primary One Registration Exercise in the preceding year. Admissions to secondary schools, on the other hand, are conducted by the MOE in an annual "posting" exercise whereby pupils who have passed their Primary School Leaving Examination (PSLE) are posted to a secondary school based on their PSLE results and their choice of schools.

Because there are many secondary schools to choose from, posting or admission to a school of choice depends on meeting qualifying criteria for admission set by the schools and on the availability of places. Generally, though, secondary schools with affiliated primary schools give students of the affiliated schools priority for admission.

There are no anti-discrimination laws per se in Singapore. Even so, the MOE has implemented policies to prevent discrimination based on where school admissions are concerned. For example, attendance at religious activities cannot be set as a condition for students to be admitted to a school.

This policy affects "mission" or religious-based schools and is successfully implemented in Singapore because most of these schools are heavily funded by the government. Thus, the conditions schools can impose for admission are limited considerably by MOE's requirements.

Students with Special Needs

Singapore is a signatory to the United Nations Convention on the Rights of the Child (UNCRC, 1989). In response to Article 23, which protects the rights of children with disabilities to have access to and receive education, the government has initiated policies rather than legislation to fulfill its obligation. In fact, children with special needs are exempted from compulsory education altogether.

Singapore's approach to special education is to implement a shared responsibility among communities, the government, and the family (Teh, 2011). Special Education Schools[19] (SPED schools) are set up by voluntary welfare organizations, and are registered as private schools under the Education Act. Funding for these schools is shared equally between the MOE and the National Council of Social Services.

Children with disabilities are not required by law to attend regular schools. Yet children with mild special educational and behavioral needs, for example, dyslexia and attention deficit hyperactivity disorder, are commonly integrated into the mainstream system. This is because mainstream schools provide support in the form of "Allied Educators for Learning and Behavioural Support" and teachers trained in special needs. Allied educators (similar to teacher aides), work with qualified teachers in the instruction and interaction with pupils, and are equipped with specific skills in reading, spelling, socialization and organization.

Singapore has taken gargantuan steps to enhance support for children with disabilities and integrate them into mainstream schools, compared with the position twenty-five to thirty years ago, when their needs were left largely to voluntary welfare groups. The next step forward would be to make education compulsory for this group of children. As Teh pointed out in 2011 (p. 188), some parents do not send their children to SPED schools because of the costs. Hence, the argument that "the enforcement of compulsory education on parents of such children may be unduly harsh" can be overcome by making education at SPED schools free for such children, just as education is free for children in the mainstream schools.

Discipline

Discipline in schools is strictly governed by MOE policies and a part of the Principal's Handbook which is not accessible to the public. Singapore, as an Asian country, places great importance on respect for elders as well as social status. Put another way, the MOE expects classroom environments to be marked by respect for teachers such that any disrespect by students toward their teachers is considered a serious disciplinary offense. All schools set out rules and regulations stipulating types of behavior that are deemed to be misconduct and the consequences for breaching the rules (Teh, 2015).

If misconduct is considered serious, school authorities impose severe disciplinary measures, including corporal punishment,[20] suspension, and expulsion. The MOE requires punishment to be complemented with counseling and follow-up guidance (Ministry of Education, 2014). Corporal punishment, suspension, and expulsion are to be used as last resort measures, usually where the offenses are serious and the consequences explicitly stated in a school's discipline policy. Suspension or expulsions are only administered where they are necessary to signal to students that their (mis)behaviors are clearly unacceptable or where their (mis)behavior undermines school discipline or threatens the safety of other students.

In accessing the information available on the MOE website, there is no mention of the term "due process" in the disciplinary procedures. There appears to be an assumption that, once school rules are broken or where serious misconduct has occurred, educators have the prerogative to impose punishment. The only procedure required of school authorities is to inform the parents of the students of what happened and to explain the reasons for the suspension or expulsion of their children and the exact duration for which these sanctions last.

Search and Seizure/Drug Testing

Singapore has one of the strictest set of laws internationally on drug-related offenses, governed by the Misuse of Drugs Act (Cap 185)(the MDA Act). In Singapore, the possession, consumption, manufacturing, import, export, or trafficking of these and other controlled drugs in any amount are illegal. Persons caught with drugs could face the death penalty, caning, and/or life imprisonment.

Under the MDA Act, any officer of the bureau, police officers above the rank of Assistant Superintendent of Police, or any polices officer authorized by this official, may, at any time, search premises and individuals without search warrants, if they "reasonably suspects that there is to be found a controlled drug or article liable to seizure" (Section 24 of the MDA Act). Section 31 of the MDA act also allows authorized officers to demand urinalysis of suspected drug offenders.

However, the situation of students experimenting with controlled drugs is virtually unheard of in Singapore, given the difficulties in securing them. Nonetheless, there are mentions in the principal's handbook of a different kind of abuse, namely, inhalant abuse. Guidelines on managing inhalant abuse are described therein, along with measures to help such students.

Freedom of Religion in Prayer and Dress

Because Singapore is a secular country, the question of religion is not a matter of concern to schools unless they have religious affiliations. Such schools request permission from the MOE to establish and maintain their schools for the education of children and to provide instruction in its own religion. There are Christian schools, such as Anglican, Methodist, Roman Catholic, and Presbyterian; Islamic religious schools; and a Buddhist primary school.

Religious schools are required to practice religious tolerance wherein students can be exempted from religious lessons if their parents wish to withdraw them from these classes. Students, therefore, arguably enjoy religious freedom in Singapore insofar as being able to attend religious schools of their choice.

Students in Islamic schools are also able to conform to the Muslim dress code. The controversy over religious freedom occurs when Muslim students are enrolled in government schools. This is because, under MOE's policies, headscarves are not permitted in public schools. In 2002, four primary one girls were suspended from school because they insisted on wearing headscarves to school (Koh, 2013). Although the MOE's policy has not changed, the debate on this issue is still ensuing today.

Freedom of speech

According to Articles 12 and 13 of the UNCRC, "States Parties shall assure to the child who is capable of forming his or her own views the rights to express those views freely in all matters affecting the child . . . the child shall have the right to freedom of expression." The Committee on the Rights of the Child in 2003 reported that Singapore had taken the welcome step of opening up avenues for students to express themselves freely through forums, seminars, and debates at different levels (UN Committee on the Rights of the Child, 2003a).

Behind all of the rhetoric, though, lies much doubt in people's minds about the topics of conversation. Noncontroversial issues, such as whether students are allowed to carry mobile phones to school or the types of extracurricular activities students should participate in, are hardly the diet of fundamental change. Where true freedom of expression exists, life is never quite so comfortable.

In July 2015, a sixteen-year-old male student received a four-week jail sentence for uploading a video on YouTube insulting the late Lee Kuan Yew, former Prime Minister of Singapore. In the video, the student criticized Lee for the poverty, income inequality, and lack of civil liberties in Singapore along with comparing him with Stalin, Hitler, and Jesus, stating "They are both power hungry, malicious and deceive others into thinking that they are compassionate and kind" (Simmons, 2015). The student was charged with, and found guilty of, "deliberate intention of wounding the religious feelings of Christians" under s 298 of the Singapore Penal Code.

One might question the political overtone of this case, even though the insult against former PM Lee was not pursued, but this is a clear example of how far free speech can realistically go in Singapore. Although it is understandable that there should be laws to prevent the incitement of religious hatred, some might argue that arresting a sixteen-year-old who made a video in his own bedroom was perhaps too drastic a reaction. It is not surprising, therefore, that this episode attracted criticisms from abroad that Singapore has failed to respect the right to freedom of expression.[21]

EMERGING ISSUES

An emerging issue in Singapore is the state of free speech. The rights to freedom of expression are not absolute insofar as they can be curtailed by parliament in the form of legislation. Yet younger Singaporeans are widely exposed to social media and the Internet where the stand for human rights is frequently championed. As such, the young will likely view the restrictions on free speech imposed by the government as a breach of their human rights.

Also, the government and school leaders are likely to be put under pressure to shift from an authoritarian to a more consultative leadership style. Still, while there is a need to give more avenues for freedom of expression, as an Asian country, respect for authority and others in the community are societal and are cultural expectations that will not be easily discarded.

Another emerging issue in Singapore concerns the admission of students to foreign schools. International schools provide parents an alternative to national schools and normative education. Yet the MOE regulates Singapore Citizen (SC) admission to Foreign System Schools (FSS) so that, in effect, the opportunity for choice is extremely limited.

SCs seeking admission into FSS must be individually approved by MOE, and each case is decided according to a set of cabinet-approved criteria. Further, SCs cannot comprise more than 10 percent of the total enrollment in any international school. This has led some unfortunate situations where, for example, a student who has a mild disability and who is not suited to a SPED school was unable to enroll in an international school with special needs expertise.

There may not be many emerging issues touching on rights in Singapore. Still, one is conscious that globalization will expose students, teachers, and parents to systems of education in the West as well as the rights of their overseas counterparts. This may well lead them to compare and contrast their relative freedoms, resulting in Singapore's facing increasing challenges to existing attitudes and policies.

CONCLUSION

To Green (1997, p. 147), Singapore's education system was not only instrumental in its "miraculous economic development but equally a vehicle for promoting a civic identity, based on the ideological tripod of multiculturalism, multilingualism and meritocracy." The legal framework for education in Singapore certainly played a large part in this success. The adoption of the English language as the medium of instruction, making bilingualism compulsory in school, together with the regulatory interventions under the Education Act, ensured that the nation is not fragmented by differing educational experiences.

This chapter traced the sources of education law in Singapore and the institutional issues surrounding primary and secondary education. While there are rights conferred on both teachers and students, not many are entrenched in legislation. The rights provided in the Constitution are very broadly stated and subject to interpretation by the courts, as seen in *Public Prosecutor v. Taw Cheng Kong* (1998), discussed above. Thus, many of the issues discussed here concern policies and procedure, and Singapore has made considerable progress in formulating policies to tackle faculty rights and student rights. Although the pieces of legislation affecting education in Singapore are modest compared with Western countries, the need for education law will continue to grow simply because education has played, and will continue to play, a central role in shaping the country.

NOTES

1. See American Institute for Research (2005), where Singaporean students ranked first in the world on the Trends in International Mathematics and Science Study 2003. See also Mourshed et al. (2010) where Singapore has journeyed from "good to great" and was ranked as a "sustained improver" over the course of five years or more.
2. Under Article 12(1) of the Singapore Constitution, all persons are equal before the law and entitled to the equal protection of the law.
3. Article 16 ensures that there is no discrimination against any citizen of Singapore on the grounds of religion, race, descent, and/or place of birth in the administration of any educational institution maintained by a public authority. It also prohibits discrimination in the providing of funds in the form of public authority financial aid for the maintenance or education of pupils or students in any educational institution regardless of whether it is maintained by a public authority and whether it is within or outside Singapore.
4. Education Endowment and Savings Schemes (Amendment) Act 2014. (No. 33 of 2014).
5. These guidelines are found in the Principal's Handbook provided by the Ministry of Education, Singapore, to all principals.
6. Statistics show a 95 percent participation rate of children aged 6 in primary 1 (Gopinathan, 1995).

7. These are government schools, government-aided schools, independent schools, or other such other schools as may be prescribed.

8. Parents who homeschool their children and religious schools have to prepare their children or students for the national primary school leaving examination, just like other mainstream schools.

9. The public expenditure on education consists of current and capital public expenditure on education. This includes government spending on educational institutions (both public and private), education administration as well as subsidies for private entities (students/households and other privates entities).

10. Students who are considered to have mild special educational needs are supported in mainstream schools.

11. The specialized independent schools are National University of Singapore High School of Mathematics and Science, School of Science and Technology, School of the Arts, and Singapore Sports School.

12. This information was provided to the first author orally by legal officers in the Legal Department, Ministry of Education. Prior to September 11, 2007, there were no reported cases of lawsuits against schools for negligence.

13. In *UY v. Attorney General*, the eleven-year-old male plaintiff was at an audition for a school concert and was running to the toilet when he slipped and fell, and hit his leg against a pipe along the corridor. He fractured his left thigh bone which eventually led to a shortening of the limb. The plaintiff alleged that the school failed to ensure the floor was dry at all times, failed to supervise students properly and failed to ensure that the school premises were safe at all times. The plaintiff did not succeed because he failed to prove the defendant breached its duty of care.

14. For example in 2010, the father of a student who died during a school mountain trek alleged that the school's medical response to the student's illness was inadequate, and in the same year, a teacher sued the MOE over an injury she sustained when she had to climb through a ventilation opening after finding herself locked inside a school building.

15. Remunerations are compatible with beginning lawyers, engineers and even medical doctors in the government service.

16. The MOE puts aside $2,000 to $4,800 each year for every eligible education officer.

17. The other teachers' unions are the Singapore Chinese Teachers' Union, the Singapore Tamil Teachers' Union, and the Singapore Malay Teachers' Union.

18. Section 377A of the Penal Code states "Any male person who, in public or private, commits, or abets the commission of, or procures or attempts to procure the commission by any male person of, any act of gross indecency with another male person, shall be punished with imprisonment for a term which may extend to 2 years."

19. As of January 2010, there are twenty special education schools catering to various disability groups. See http://www.moe.gov.sg/education/special-education/schoollist/ for the schools and the groups they cater to.

20. As permitted under section 88 of the Education (Schools) Regulation.

21. Rupert Abbott, South East Asia and Pacific Research Director at Amnesty International said, "Amos Yee is not a criminal. He should never have been charged, let alone convicted. He has been punished solely for exercising his right to freedom of expression." https://www.amnesty.org/en/latest/news/2015/07/singapore-amos-yee-sentence-a-dark-day-for-freedom-of-expression/.

REFERENCES

American Institutes for Research (January 2005). *What the United States can learn from Singapore's world-class mathematics system: An exploratory study.*

Arnold, W. (2003, July 4). "Quietly, Singapore lifts its ban on hiring gays." *International Herald Tribune.*

CIA World FactBook. 2014/2015, Vol. 52, p. 664–67. 4p., Database: MasterFILE Premier.

Chan, J. (2007). "Language, law and education: From colony to nation." Keynote speaker at the 16th Annual Australia and New Zealand Education Law Association Conference, Hervey Bay, Australia, September 26–28. Conference theme: *Contention and controversy in education law*.

Chong, T. (2010). "Introduction: The role of success in Singapore's national identity." In T. Chong (eds.), *Management of success: Singapore revisited* (pp. 1–18). Singapore: Institute of Southeast Asian Studies Publishing.

Contact Singapore (2015), "Facts & figures, Singapore information," https://www.contactsingapore.sg/en/professionals/why-singapore/about-singapore/facts-and-figures.

Goh, C. B. and Gopinathan, S. (2008). "The development of education in Singapore since 1965." In Lee, S. K., Goh, C. B., Fredriksen, B., and Tan, J. P. (2008). (eds.). *Toward a better future: Education and training for economic development in Singapore since 1965* (pp. 12–38). The International Bank for Reconstruction and Development/The World Bank.

Goh, C. B. and Lee, S. K. (2008). "Making teacher education responsive and relevant." In Lee, S. K., Goh, C. B., Fredriksen, B., and Tan, J. P. (2008). (eds.). *Toward a better future: Education and training for economic development in Singapore since 1965* (pp. 96–113). The International Bank for Reconstruction and Development/The World Bank.

Gopinathan, S. (1995). "Education and development in Singapore." In Morriss, P. and Sweeting, A. (eds.), *Education and development in East Asia* (pp. 79–103). New York: Garland Publishing.

Green, A. (1997). *Education, globalization and the nation state*. Basingstoke, UK: Macmillan

Gwee, Y. H. and Doraisamy, T. R. (1969). *150 years of education in Singapore*. Singapore: TTC Publications Board, Teachers' Training College.

Koh, J. (2013) *Parliamentary Replies: Government Expenditure*. Retrieved from http://www.moe.gov.sg/media/parliamentary-replies/2013/10/government-expenditure-on-education.php.

Koh, X. H. (2013). DPM Teo weighs in on debate; PM Lee Hsien Loong, Yaacob meet Malay PAP MPs, at http://www.todayonline.com/singapore/hijab-issue-govt-must-balance-community-requirements.

Lee, E. (2008). *Singapore: The Unexpected Nation*. Institute of Southeast Asian Studies.

Lee, R. (2003, June 12). "Remake S'pore? Start with yourself first; take the lead and don't always rely on the govt." *The Straits Times, Singapore*, p. 5.

Lee, S. K., Goh, C. B., Fredriksen, B. & Tan, J. P. (2008). (eds.). *Toward a better future: Education and training for economic development in Singapore since 1965*. The International Bank for Reconstruction and Development/The World Bank.

Lum, S. (2011, February 2). "Fall in school: Teacher and MOE reach agreement." *The Straits Times, Singapore*.

Ministry of Education (2014). *Forum Letter Replies: MOE and schools are committed to maintaining high standards of discipline in schools.* http://www.moe.gov.sg/media/forum/2014/05/maintaining-high-standards-of-discipline.php.

Ministry of Education. *Applying to be a Teacher.* http://www.moe.gov.sg/careers/teach/applying/.

Ministry of Education. *Choosing the Right School: A Parent's Guide for Children with Special Educational Needs.* http://www.moe.gov.sg/education/special-education/files/parents-guide-children-special-educational-needs.pdf.

Ministry of Education. *Enhancing your strengths — Career Tracks.* http://www.moe.gov.sg/careers/teach/career-info/.

Ministry of Education. *Forum Letter Replies: No proselytization allowed in schools*. http://www.moe.gov.sg/media/forum/2005/20051025a.htm.

Ministry of Education. (2013). *Highlights from Education Dialogue Sessions: June–July 2013.* http://www.moe.gov.sg/our-singapore-conversation/files/highlights-phase2-educators-dialogue.pdf.

Ministry of Education. (2012). *Parliamentary Replies: Criteria for suspension of students from schools.* http://www.moe.gov.sg/media/parliamentary-replies/2012/05/criteria-for-suspension-of-students.php.

Ministry of Education. *Secondary School Education*. http://www.moe.gov.sg/education/secondary/files/secondary-school-education-booklet.pdf.
Ministry of Education. *Special Education in Singapore*. http://www.moe.gov.sg/education/special-education.
Ministry of Education. *The Singapore Education Journey*. http://www.moe.gov.sg/education/landscape.
Ministry of Education. *Teacher-Student Relationships*. http://www.moe.gov.sg/media/parliamentary-replies/2012/01/teacher-student-relationships.php.
Ministry of Finance (2014). *Analysis of Revenue and Expenditure—Financial Year 2014*. Retrieved from http://www.singaporebudget.gov.sg/data/budget_2014/download/FY2014_Analysis_of_Revenue_and_Expenditure.pdf.
Ministry of Finance (2015). *Analysis of Revenue and Expenditure—Financial Year 2015*. Retrieved from http://www.singaporebudget.gov.sg/data/budget_2015/download/FY2015_Analysis_of_Revenue_and_Expenditure.pdf.
Mourshed M., Chijioke C., and Barber, M. *How the world's most improved school systems keep getting better*. Report. McKinsey & Company, 2010.
Ng, P. T. (2007). "Quality assurance in the Singapore education system in an era of diversity and innovation." *Educational Research for Policy & Practice*, 6(3), 235–47.
Public Prosecutor v Taw Cheng Kong [1998] SGCA 37.
Simmons, J. (2015). "Lee Kuan Yew is Finally Dead!" blogger prosecuted. http://freespeechdebate.com/en/case/lee-kuan-yew-is-finally-dead-blogger-prosecuted/.
Singapore's Open Data Portal (2015). *Government Expenditure on Education (Graph Data)*. Retrieved from https://data.gov.sg/dataset/government-expenditure-on-education-total.
Singapore Statutes Online (2015). *Misuse of Drugs Act*. Retrieved from http://statutes.agc.gov.sg/aol/search/display/view.w3p;page=0;query=DocId%3A%22c13adadb-7d1b-45f8-a3bb-92175f83f4f5%22%20Status%3Apublished%20Depth%3A0;rec=0.
Tan, B. and Teh, M. K. (2013). "Singapore." In Russo, C. J. (ed.) *Handbook of comparative higher education law* (pp. 275–90). Lanham, MD: Rowman & Littlefield.
Teh, M. K. (2011). "Singapore." In C. J. Russo (ed.) *The legal rights of students with disabilities: International perspectives* (pp. 179–93). Lanham, MD: Rowman & Littlefield.
Teh, M. K. (2015). "The Changing Shape of Misdemeanor in Singapore Schools." In C. J. Russo (ed.) *Global Interest in Student Behavior* (pp. 51–67). Lanham, MD: Rowman & Littlefield.
Teh, M. K. and Chia S. M. (2012). "Singapore." In Glenn C. L., De Groof, J., and Candal, C. S. (eds.) *Balancing freedom, autonomy, and accountability in education, volume 4* (pp. 227–38). The Netherlands: Wolf Legal Publishers.
Teh, M.K. and Stott K. (2009). "Singapore." In Russo, C. J. and De Groof, J. (eds.) *The employment rights of teachers: Exploring education law worldwide* (pp. 173–187). Lanham, MD: Rowman and Littlefield.
Thio, L. (2012). "Between apology and apogee, autochthony: The "rule of law" beyond the rules of law in Singapore." *Singapore Journal of Legal Studies*, 269–97, 276.
Turnbull, C. (1977). *A history of Singapore 1819–1975*. Kuala Lumpur: Oxford University Press.
UN Committee on the Rights of the Child (CRC), *UN Committee on the Rights of the Child: State Party Report: Singapore*, 17 March 2003, CRC/C/51/Add.8, available at: http://www.refworld.org/docid/3f8d161d4.html (accessed November 7, 2015).
UNESCO Institute of Statistics (2015) *Education: Expenditure on Education as % of GDP (from Government Sources)*. Retrieved from http://data.uis.unesco.org/index.aspx?queryid=181&lang=en.
United Nations Convention on the Rights of the Child 1989. Retrieved from http://www.ohchr.org/en/professionalinterest/pages/crc.aspx.
UY v. Attorney General (2007) SGDC 255.
Viyayan, K. C. (October 20, 2010). "Father sues school over daughter's death." *The Straits Times*. http://thecourtroom.stomp.com.sg/courtroom/cases/father-sues-tkgs-over-daughters-death-in-mountain-trek.

Weiss, Meredith L. (2015). *Singapore lifts ban on hiring lesbian and gay employees*. Salem Press Encyclopedia.
World Bank (2015), Singapore, http://data.worldbank.org/country/singapore.

LEGISLATION

Compulsory Education Act (Chapter 51) 2003.
Constitution of the Republic of Singapore 1965.
Constitution of the Republic of Singapore, Article 116(1), Public Service (Disciplinary Proceedings) Regulations.
Constitution of the Republic of Singapore, Article 116(3), Public Service Commission (Delegation of Disciplinary Functions) Directions.
Education Ordinance 1957, No. 45 of 1957, Colony of Singapore Ordinances.
Education Act (Cap. 87).
Education Endowment and Savings Schemes Act (Chapter 87A).
Education Endowment and Savings Schemes (Amendment) Act 2014.
Education (Grant-in-Aid) Regulations 1983.
Education Service Incentive Payment Act 2001 (Chapter 87B).
G.N. No. S 2/58—Education (Schools) Regulations 1957; Grant-in-Aid Regulations 1957, Colony of Singapore Government Gazette Supp. No. 98/1957.
Misuse of Drugs Act (Cap 185).
Private Education Act (Cap 247A).
School Boards Incorporation Act 1990 (Chapter 284A).

Chapter Five

Analysis and Reflections

Charles J. Russo

INTRODUCTION

As important as education is, individuals cannot assert this right absent the existence of legal systems establishing effective school systems under the law. As such, respect for basic rights such as teaching and learning is a long-established tenet in most countries. Thus, in all four of the countries covered in this book, Australia, Malaysia, New Zealand, and Singapore, both students and teachers have an array of rights that are explicitly identified and protected in varying degrees.

The leaders in the education law systems described in this volume strive to meet the duties as assigned by their national governments or decentralized public authorities in their provinces, states and/or territories. Moreover, educational law, and its accompanying policies, is a topic of intense public concern, regardless of whether it is governed centrally at the national level or more locally at the provincial, state, or territorial level. The fundamental roles of teachers in these systems, namely providing education to the children in their classes, is thus rightly seen as a key component of their governments as they charged with the duty of public service and protecting the common good by helping to shape educated citizens.

It is important to keep in mind that national systems described throughout this volume, combined with the statutory basis embedded in a human rights culture, are indispensable for the creation of an effective teaching and learning environment. However, this appears to be only one side of the coin. On the flip side of the coin, it is equally as important to bear in mind that as important as the law is, teaching and learning takes place in classrooms, not in legislative chambers or courtrooms. Education is thus essentially a social science founded on the dynamics of sound relationships and mutual respect that must occur in environments where all share the interest of providing the holistic common good for children and society.

SUMMARY AND ANALYSIS

In order to provide a sense of what this book is all about this section briefly reviews similarities and differences in the national education law systems described in this volume.

Legal Systems

Without saying so directly, all of the legal systems the four nations described in the volume seek to apply what can broadly be described as the rule of law with well-developed or emerging series of laws addressing education.

Not surprisingly, Australia, Malaysia, New Zealand, and Singapore, in light of their histories as British Commonwealth nations, have systems most closely resembling the Anglo-American model which relies on common law and written constitutions. Even so, there is scant reported litigation on education law in almost all of the countries reported on in this volume.

Institutional Issues

Compulsory Attendance

All of the nations reviewed in this book starting no later than age six, lasting for varying periods of time and with differing degrees of responsibility to ensure that parents send their children to school, whether public or non-public. Further, Australia and Singapore explicitly recognize homeschooling as an option.

As to compulsory attendance, starting typically at the age of five, children in Australia must remain in school until they turn sixteen or seventeen, depending on the state or territory. Similarly, children in New Zealand must attend school between the ages of from six and sixteen. Compulsory schooling ends at sixteen. Children in Singapore must attend schools between the ages of six and fifteen. In Malaysia children must attend through the completion of elementary school or sixth grade.

School Funding and Types: Public and Non-public

Nations around the world, including this reviewed in this volume, recognize a wide variety of types of schools. Australia, New Zealand, and Singapore provide varying levels of funding for both government and nongovernment schools, including those that are religiously affiliated. Further, New Zealand has recently started providing funding for charter schools. On the other hand,

Malaysia restricts funding to state schools. At the same time, all of the nations discussed in the book are home to a variety of public and non-public schools whether religious or internationally based with the latter serving children of diplomats and residential expats.

Governance

A wide variety of governance models exist in the nations in this book, from highly centralized to decentralized models of governance and control. In Australia, although this model is not universal, depending on the state or territory, regardless of whether they are government or nongovernment schools, governance is undertaken by representative school councils or boards made up of the school principal, teachers, parents, community members, and, in limited cases, student representatives. There is generally no legal requirement to include students on a school council.

Further, Malaysian law requires all schools, whether private or national to create governing boards to manage their activities. Similarly, in New Zealand, where all schools are autonomous, control and management is vested in boards of trustees for individual schools. Conversely, Singapore is managed primarily by its Ministry of Education which directs the formulation and implementation of educational policies while controlling the development and administration of government or government-aided private or non-public primary schools, and secondary schools.

Safety and Liability Issues

As noted in the discussion of legal systems, it should not be surprising that Australia, Malaysia, New Zealand, and Singapore, with their shared histories as British Commonwealth nations, have common law negligence systems operating fairly similarly.

Malaysia, in an interesting twist for students of the law, explicitly extends the common law doctrine of in loco parentis, "in the place of the parent," particularly with regard to younger children.

In what is certainly a sign of the times, along with the fact that all of the nations have a variety of nondiscrimination laws in place to safeguard students and teachers, they are extending their laws to cover more contemporary sources of harm to children. For example, New Zealand has taken comprehensive steps to eliminate bullying and harassment, whether in schools on via the use of technology, also known as cyberbullying, in its schools while Australia, long a leader in this area, has taken on harassment of students with disabilities. Also an emerging issue in Malaysia, lawmakers and educators are taking steps to eliminate bullying in schools.

Faculty Rights

Due Process in Employment and Dismissal

In varying degrees, the education law systems in all of the nations reviewed in this volume offer protections for teachers throughout their professional careers via a combination of statutory and common law principles. Additionally, the educational systems in all four of the systems addressed in this volume established qualifications for teachers, particularly in public schools, requiring them to meet professional standards and safeguarding their rights to employment.

Freedom of Speech

All of the countries in the book recognize the rights to freedom of speech and association in the form of creating and joining unions. Insofar as Australia has no constitutionally entrenched bill of rights, freedom of speech is found in statute and common law. The Australian Constitution does provide a limited implied right to freedom of political communication derived from the principles of responsible and representative government and hence the right to participate in political discourse.

The Malaysian Federal Constitution provides for the right to freedom of speech, assembly, and association. New Zealand's Bill of Rights Act affirms, protects, and promotes human rights and fundamental freedoms in respect of public office and public functions, including the rights to freedom of thought, conscience, religion, and expression.

Pursuant to the Constitution of Singapore, all citizens, including teachers, have the right to freedom of speech and expression. However, the government may restrict this freedom as necessary in the best interest of Singapore. Even with this freedom, teachers are expected to conduct themselves in a manner upholding the integrity of the public service. This means that teachers may have to seek consent from the Ministry of Education before agreeing to make broadcast or television appearances relating directly or indirectly to their official work.

Freedom of Association/Unions

A right closely associated with speech is freedom of association. Accordingly, teachers' unions or professional associations are present in all of the nations covered in this book and often wield considerable clout in schools. For example, laws in Malaysia, and neighboring Singapore, recognize that teachers have a right to form unions, they explicitly add that it is not absolute and can be limited in the interest of the public well-being. Further, although there is no express or independent right to freedom of association, which is regarded as a corollary to the implied right to political communication, teacher unions are present throughout Australia.

Freedom of Religion

The constitutions and/or statutes in Australia, Malaysia, New Zealand, and Singapore guarantee freedom of religion in varying degrees, occasionally allowing officials to limit its exercise so as to not engender violence and create disruptions in schools.

Protection from Discrimination

Across all jurisdictions in Australia, teachers and principals have the right not to be directly and indirectly discriminated against on the basis of various prohibited grounds, including age, disability, race, nationality, ethnicity, gender, sexual orientation, marital status, pregnancy, breastfeeding, political affiliation, and/or religious belief. The Constitution of Malaysia guarantees public school teachers, irrespective of their races, to be treated in an impartial manner. New Zealand's Rights Act forbids discrimination against teachers based on religious or ethical belief, sex, sexual orientation, color, race, ethnic, national origin, and/or disability.

Singaporean law dictates that all persons are equal before the law and entitled to the equal protection of the law. Further, it prohibits discrimination against citizens of Singapore on the grounds only of religion, race, descent, and/or place of birth in any law or in the appointment to any office or employment under a public authority.

Student Rights

Admissions and Freedom from Discrimination

All four of the education law systems covered in this book have enacted compulsory attendance laws specifying the ages at which children must enter and through which they must remain in schools. In order to ensure fair and orderly admissions processes, many of these laws also set forth anti-discrimination provisions to protect children.

A more prescriptive nation in this regard, Australian law and regulations generally focus on the ages of children their citizenship or visa status, and residential qualifications. Although there is no personal constitutional right to religious freedom in Australia, at common law students have a right to freedom of religion, thought, and conscience. Malaysia forbids discrimination against citizens, including students, on the grounds of religion, race, descent, and/or place of birth; this protection extends to admissions in schools.

New Zealand applies the full force and effect of its anti-discrimination laws to admissions, safeguarding children from discrimination due to religious or ethical belief, sex and sexual orientation, color, race, ethnic, and/or national origins. Although there is no anti-discrimination legislation per se in Singapore, its MOE has implemented policies to prevent discrimination on the ground of religion as to admission is concerned.

Freedom of Religion

Insofar as there is no personal constitutional right to religious freedom in Australia, at common law students have a right to freedom of religion, thought, and conscience. In Malaysia, insofar as parents or guardians have the right to determine their religion of their children until they turn eighteen, students do not have an absolute right to practice the religions of their choice until they attain the age of eighteen. Additionally, Malaysia has yet to ratify the provision related to religion in the United Nations Convention on the Rights of the Child.

New Zealand holds strong to a long tradition of protecting religious freedom as evidenced in a wide variety of laws. Consistent with language in the Singaporean Constitution, all persons, including students, have the right to profess and practice their religions and to propagate their beliefs.

Freedom of Speech and Expression

The Education Law systems in the four countries in this volume vary with regard to speech and expression and the related matter of whether students must wear uniforms to school regardless of their religious beliefs. Like religion there, although students in Australia lack a constitutional right to freedom of speech and expression, it is protected by the common law. The law does allow school officials to develop and enforce policies and reasonable rules on dress codes and personal appearance such as body piercings to regulate student behavior.

Disputes have arisen in New Zealand over of freedom of religion as it is connected with freedom of expression associated with religious manifestations and expressions. Because the freedoms of thought, conscience, and religion extend to the right of students to wear items such as headscarves, kirpans, crucifixes, and *taonga* school officials in New Zealand must justify any restrictions they impose in this regard.

Uniforms are mandatory in public and private elementary and secondary schools in Malaysia albeit by law in the former and school rules in the latter. In a case involving religion and expression, the Federal Court rejected a parental claim that officials violated the right freedom of religion by forbidding their daughter from wear religious headgear to school. Similarly, Singaporean law allows students in Islamic schools to conform to the Muslim dress code. However, if Muslim students attend government schools, they cannot wear headscarves. As to the spoken word, Singapore respects freedom of speech but has been engaged in legal controversies when officials limited a student's right in this regard.

Due Process and Discipline

Australia, Malaysia, New Zealand, and Singapore have enacted extensive systems of due process safeguarding the rights of students who are subject to suspension and/or expulsion from school. Under these systems, corporal punishment or caning in secondary school is permitted in Malaysia for serious disciplinary infractions by males only but is rare at the elementary level. In like manner, Singapore permits corporal punishment but only on male students. Educators can administer this punishment with light canes on the palms of the hands or on the buttocks over the clothing; still, the Ministry of Education has issued strict guidelines on how and when to administer such punishment. Australia and New Zealand expressly prohibit the use of corporal punishment.

Search and Seizure/Drug Testing

Due to growing problems associated with violence coupled with the use of weapons, drugs, and alcohol in an around schools, some nations have addressed the need to search students and/or their property as well as to subject them to drug testing. The nations with the most extensive laws in terms of enacted statutes are Australia and New Zealand.

In light of the duty of school officials to provide safe and orderly environments while caring for the health and well-being of students, Australian law permits searches of students. The power of school officials extends to mobile phones, iPads, and other such devices if they contain illegal or offensive material or if they are being used inappropriately. However, officials in government schools in Australia lack the power to test students for drugs, including breathalyzer tests, at schools or during school activities but may require students to undergo drug tests and provide medical reports as preconditions for inclusion in, for example, sports programs. Nongovernment school polices, on the other hand, may provide for drug testing.

New Zealand recognizes the right to be secure from unreasonable searches and seizures. However, school officials can require students to produce, reveal, and surrender items in their possession which are likely to endanger the safety of others, detrimentally affect learning environments, or be harmful because they pose immediate threats to the physical or emotional safety of anyone. Officials can search students' outer clothing based on the reasonable belief that harm may ensue if they do not act. Blanket searches are not allowed in any circumstances. If school officials are convinced that serious criminal offenses have been committed or are imminent, and drugs or weapons are involved, they must notify the police who can execute their usual powers in such circumstances. The law apparently does not directly address drug testing.

Singapore has one of the strictest set of laws internationally on drug related offenses, such that the possession, consumption, manufacturing, import, export, and/or trafficking of these and other controlled drugs in any amount are illegal. Persons caught with drugs could face the death penalty, caning, and/or life imprisonment. Various police officials may search individuals at any time without search warrants, if they reasonably suspect that they possess controlled drugs or articles liable to seizure. Fortunately, the situation of students experimenting with controlled drugs is virtually unheard of in Singapore due to difficulties associated with obtaining such substances.

Students with Special Needs

In dealing with children with special needs, school systems in Australia and New Zealand explicitly have adopted comprehensive structures to meet their needs in inclusive educational settings. Malaysian courts often take the best interests of students with disabilities into consideration when addressing their educational needs, highlighting that their rights to have basic educations typically should override financial considerations.

The law in Singapore does not obligate children with disabilities to attend regular schools. Still, children with mild special educational and behavioral needs are commonly integrated into the mainstream system. Further, Singapore views special education as a shared responsibility between and among communities, the government, and the families by creating Special Education Schools, established by voluntary welfare organizations.

Emerging Issues

In light of the rapid growth and development in technology, it should not be surprising that matters related to its use stands out as the primary emerging issue in the nations reviewed in this volume. Safety issues are starting to arise in Malaysia and New Zealand (as manifested in difficulties associated with search and seizure of electronic devices, cyberbullying, and sexting). In a related concern, free speech is an emerging concern in Singapore, the first of three issues, especially because students are widely exposed to social media and the Internet where the stand for human rights is frequently championed. As such, tension is likely to arise in Singapore as students chafe under the restrictions on free speech imposed by the government as a breach of their human rights. On another safety-related matter, Malaysia identified bullying as an emerging concern while seeking to stem the growing tide of student misconduct in elementary schools.

Australia identified the education of refugee and asylum-seeker children as a significant human rights' issues for schools. A different emerging issue in Singapore concerns the admission of students to international schools that provide parents with alternatives to national schools and normative education. The final emerging issues touching on rights in Singapore is the concern that globalization will expose students, teachers, and parents to systems of education in the West as well as the rights of their overseas counterparts. This contact may lead stakeholders to compare and contrast their relative freedoms, resulting in Singapore's facing increasing challenges to existing attitudes and policies.

RECOMMENDATIONS

In light of the preceding summaries on the status of the national systems of education law described in this volume, it should be evident that schooling is a fundamental human right. As such, educational, political, and civic leaders not only in the nations reviewed in this volume, but elsewhere, must act to ensure the compulsory attendance rights for all children regardless of demographic characteristics such as race, gender, and religion.

To this end, leaders must focus on developing laws and implementing policies designed to improve schooling in places where compulsory attendance laws have long been in place. Accordingly, leaders may wish to consider the following recommendations that are designed to enhance the quality of schooling.

1. Consistent with the internationally accepted norms in the various covenants, leaders must take steps to have education explicitly recognized and safeguarded as a fundamental human right for all children. In other words, all nations must develop laws and policies designed to protect and enhance the rights of all students, and educators, regardless of their ethnicity, genders, race, and/or religion. Insofar as this can be a major challenge in parts of the world that have been reluctant to extend full rights to historically underrepresented groups such as women and religious and ethnic minorities, political and educational leaders in particular must show their mettle if they are to help their citizens to reach their full potential.
2. National and local leaders must work together to provide adequate funding designed to create schools wherein teachers can provide children with world-class educations. This is especially important during a time when there is a growing cynicism about the need for education such that it must move beyond concerns over resources or capacity in order to focus on how systems can not only be funded but also be

made accessible to all. Equitable funding must cover not only construction of facilities and purchasing instructional materials but also paying salaries designed to enhance "the best and brightest" to enter the field of education as teachers and administrators. Moreover, in making certain that all regions of a country receive adequate minimum levels of resources for schools, funding mechanisms should consider providing additional allocations for more expensive locales such as cities as well as for children with intensive needs including those with disabilities and/or those who speak minority languages and need to be taught in national/majority languages so that they can adapt in educational settings.

3. Education must be treated as an integrative factor, one that can help prepare all children to become productive members of their societies rather than set them apart from one another based on ethnicity, genders, race, and/or religion.
4. Reconceptualized school systems must be open to all children wherein educators emphasize pluralistic, cross-cultural principles that respect internationally accepted norms, as well as national laws, as explicated in the various covenants discussed herein. In other words, systems must be inclusive, not exclusive.
5. Laws and policies must be enacted to meet the needs of special student populations including, but not limited to, those who are disabled, of ethnic, religious, and linguistic minorities, and/or are refugees.
6. Institutions of higher learning must enhance teacher and administrator preparation programs, ensuring that they are at the "cutting edge" of school reform so that they can best help to educate children.
7. Leaders should adopt proactive roles in helping to create shared values among all groups in developing educational curricular/standards. It is essential for officials in central governmental ministries to maintain leadership roles in education to ensure that policies and practices are adopted uniformly in all schools and areas of their countries.
8. Educators must develop curricula, and accompanying texts, drafted primarily by appropriate professionals who can call on outside experts for assistance. Individuals from the respective governmental and educational ministries as well as from the higher education sector should provide leadership on this important project. Even as educational leaders work to develop curricula with an eye toward primarily satisfying what can be described as national needs, they must simultaneously challenge students to develop critical thinking skills befitting individuals who are preparing to assume roles as full citizens.
9. Leaders should implement curricula that all can accept. Educational leaders should also provide some consideration for ways of permitting minority and ethnic groups to preserve their independent heritages in

the schools by being open to incorporating elements of their perspectives into curricula.

10. Members of committees assigned the task of developing curricular materials should be selected from among a broad representation of stakeholders, including, but not limited to parents, students, teachers, civil leaders, interested in helping to ensure equal educational opportunities for all children.
11. Leaders, particularly in developing nations, should schedule conferences/meetings on the right to schooling in an attempt to obtain input from all parties, again including but not limited to parents, students, teachers, and civil leaders who are interested in helping to ensure equal educational opportunities for all children. In developed nations, educational leaders in particular should encourage parents to become more involved in the education of their children and citizens to vote to ensure that their school boards or governing bodies truly represent community interests while holding to appropriate educational standards.
12. In light of the rapid pace at which change occurs, leaders should regularly reevaluate and update educational goals to keep them current.

CONCLUSION

As growing interdependence between and among nations shrinks the world community, a major challenge facing civic, educational, and political leaders is ensuring the educational rights of all children. Moreover, insofar as human dignity is closely related to the protection of the physical and mental well-being of students as they grow to become productive members of their societies, the quality of the education available to them is key to the reduction and elimination of adult illiteracy and poverty in future generations.

Given the importance that education has assumed in the twenty-first century, it all but goes without saying that improvements in basic schooling for all children are a prerequisite to sustainable personal and social development. In fact, individuals are ultimately unable to exercise their fundamental social, civil, economic, and political rights unless they have received an adequate basic education. To the extent that education is a lasting investment in the future of children, indeed of society itself, as well as sustainable development and social progress in general, it is critical to improving the lives of all helping them both to break the cycle of poverty and to lead lives of full participation in democratic societies.

In the words of the United States Supreme Court, insofar as "education is perhaps the most important function of state and local governments,"[1] it is imperative for civic, educational, and political leaders to ensure that the educational rights of students remain protected as a basic component of their fundamental human rights. As daunting as the crucial challenge of safeguarding educational rights may be, it is one all leaders should welcome as they seek to build a better tomorrow for all children and their societies at large.

Aware of the need for schooling, then, this book (and its companion volumes) has striven to cover a wide array of aspects in the education laws in the K–12 systems in the four nations examined in this volume. Most nations recognize that students and teachers in general have legal rights to freedom from discrimination as well as to freedom of speech, religion, and association. Yet the legal systems in some of the countries restrict some of these rights to protect the public or national order.

The aim of these volumes is to shed light on the rights, duties, and new challenges on education law systems while highlighting the importance of respecting education as a fundamental right. As such, I hope these books will contribute to and provide a new impetus in the debate on the status of K–12 education worldwide. Inspired by what the contributors have written, together we hope that lawmakers, policy makers, and educational leaders can proceed to outline new visions of developments for the rights of students and teachers culminating in increased student achievement even if these changes are driven by national, rather than international, priorities.

NOTE

1. *Brown v. Board of Education*, 347 U.S. 483, 493 (1954).

Index

About the Editor

Charles J. Russo, MDiv, JD, EdD, is the Joseph Panzer Chair in Education in the School of Education and Health Sciences, director of its PhD program in educational leadership, and research professor of law in the School of Law at the University of Dayton. The 1998–1999 president of the (American) Education Law Association, and 2002 recipient of its McGhehey (Achievement) Award, he received a PhD Honoris Causa from Potchefstroom University, now the Potchefstroom Campus of Northwest University, in Potchefstroom, South Africa, in May 2004, for his contributions to the field of education law. Russo authored or coauthored more than 280 articles in peer-reviewed journals; authored, coauthored, edited, or coedited sixty-two books, including this volume, and more than 1,000 publications. He has spoken extensively on issues in education law in the United States and twenty-nine other nations.

About the Contributors

Sook Chia is the head of programme (education) at the School of Human Development and Social Sciences at SIM University in Singapore. Prior to joining SIM University, she worked in the Ministry of Education as an educational researcher. Her research interests include education policy, curriculum and instruction, and quality assurance in higher education.

Joan Squelch is a professor in the School of Law at the University of Notre Dame, Australia (Fremantle). She holds qualifications in education and law, and is admitted as a lawyer in the Supreme Court of New South Wales. She teachers constitutional law, administrative law, and employment law. Squelch's research interests include legal education, education and the law, education and human rights law, workplace bullying, and school governance.

Mui Kim Teh, LLB (Hons.), PhD, is both a lawyer and an educator. She is a qualified barrister-at-law in London, and qualified as an advocate and solicitor of the Supreme Court of Singapore in 1996. Teh was a lawyer in Singapore before moving to Australia. Earlier in her career, she was both a teacher and a head of department in Singapore schools. She is the recipient of the inaugural Dr. Ann Shorten Doctoral Thesis Award 2009 given by the Australia and New Zealand Education Law Association for the most outstanding PhD thesis in education law. Teh is currently based at Deakin University in Victoria, Australia, where she lectures in law.

Fatt Hee Tie, LLB (Hons), LLM, SJD, is a professor at the Faculty of Law, University of Malaya in Kuala Lumpur, Malaysia. He has taught in two secondary schools and a teachers training college for twelve years. He has also taught education law at the Faculty of Education and the Institute of

Educational Leadership for more than eighteen years. Tie is qualified as a lawyer of the High Court of Malaya. He is currently teaching law at the University of Malaya in Malaysia.

Sally Varnham is a professor with the Faculty of Law at the University of Technology Sydney (UTS). From 2011 to 2014 she was chair of the University Academic Board and remains a member of the UTS Council. Her main research interest is in legal issues arising in compulsory and higher education and her theses for LLM and PhD are in this area. She is a coeditor of *Higher Education and the Law* (2015), the first Australian book in this area and coauthor, with Professor Jim Jackson, of *Law for Educators: School and University Law in Australia* (2007). She is widely published in Australia, New Zealand, the UK, and Europe and regularly presents at national and international conferences. Varnham is a past president and director of the Australia and New Zealand Education Law Association (ANZELA).

Lightning Source UK Ltd.
Milton Keynes UK
UKOW04n1425061117
312294UK00001B/5/P

9 781475 821673